WRITING COMEDY

'Along with a rich father-in-law, a good suit, curiosity, venom and inno-cence, there is nothing a young man or woman contemplating writing tele-vision comedy needs more than Ronnie Wolfe's indispensable book.'

Frank Muir

Packed with hints, tips and warnings, here is the complete guide through the minefield of comedy writing. Experienced scriptwriter Ronald Wolfe reveals the secrets of the trade.

Sharing his success with the reader, Ronald Wolfe explains how to get started in the business and how to present your ideas in an impressive way.

He explains the different techniques required for TV, radio, stage and film, and includes sound advice on working methods. Maurice Gran and Laurence Marks, creators and writers of *Birds of a Feather*, discuss their experiences of team-writing.

The book is full of good advice from such top scriptwriters as Carla Lane of *Bread*, Jack Rosenthal, Barry Cryer and Alan Plater. Ray Galton recalls writing *Hancock's Half Hour*, and Andy Hamilton tells how he and Guy Jenkin created *Drop the Dead Donkey*, and Ian Brown, one of the writing team, tells of the American-style team-writing of *My Family*.

Is it harder for women to break into comedy? Experience and advice are given by Beryl Vertue, executive producer of *Men Behaving Badly* and *Coupling*.

Actors such as Tony Robinson and Warren Mitchell reflect on their experience of working with comedy writers, and producers and directors. Robin Nash, former BBC head of comedy, and Micheál Jacob, editor of BBC comedy development, explain how they develop the talent of new writers.

Crammed with examples from the scripts of well-known series and crisp analysis of comic formulae, *Writing Comedy* is a book every comedy scriptwriter will value.

Ronald Wolfe has been a comedy writer practically all his working life. He has written for feature films, stage shows, radio series and (in partnership with Ronald Chesney) has scripted over 500 episodes of television situation comedy. Amongst others he helped create the classic comedies The Rag Trade *and* On the Buses. *He has worked extensively abroad, for all the major networks in the USA, and in Canada, Australia, Scandinavia and Holland. He is a visiting lecturer in writing TV comedy at the City University, London, and regularly speaks at SitCom workshops run by the BFI on the South Bank; the National Film and TV School, Beaconsfield; University of Kent School of Drama, Film and Visual Arts; London Department of New York University; University of Barcelona, Spain; KomedyHaus, Hamburg, Germany; and the Writers' Summer School, Swanwick. He lives in Temple Fortune, North London.*

KA 0302694 9

Writing Comedy

A Guide to Scriptwriting for TV, Radio, Film and Stage

RONALD WOLFE

ROBERT HALE · LONDON

© *Ronald Wolfe 1992, 1996 and 2003*
First published in Great Britain 1992
This revised edition 2003

ISBN 978 0 7090 7413 7

Robert Hale Limited
Clerkenwell House
Clerkenwell Green
London EC1R 0HT

4 6 8 10 9 7 5 3

Printed and bound in Great Britain by
Biddles Limited, King's Lynn

Contents

For my wife Rose . . . for so dutifully typing my scripts and laughing at my jokes. And for our daughters, Kathryn and Debbie Joanne without whose suggestions this book would have been finished years ago.

Acknowledgements

I am deeply indebted to Ronald Chesney, my writing partner for so many years, for his permission to use extracts from scripts we wrote together.

I am also indebted to Carla Lane, Victoria Wood, Ray Galton & Alan Simpson, David Croft, Jeremy Lloyd and Jimmy Perry for permission to use extracts from their scripts.

Gratitude and thanks to the following for giving so generously their time and help: Maurice Gran & Laurence Marks, Alan Plater, Brian Cooke, Barry Cryer, Johnny Speight, Tony Robinson, Warren Mitchell, Jack Rosenthal, Humphrey Barclay, Susan Belbin, Mandy Fletcher, John Esmonde & Bob Larbey, Rosie Bunting, Andy Hamilton, Ian Brown, Micheál Jacob and Beryl Vertue.

Author's Note

I thought it best to start with a list of some of my credits, because it is on this work experience that the book is based.

1955/60
Head writer of the hit radio series Educating Archie, a series originally created and written by Eric Sykes.

This series ran until 1960. There were over two hundred episodes, and an Australian tour in 1957. The cast, at various times, included such names as Tony Hancock, Max Bygraves, Beryl Reid, Harry Secombe, Benny Hill and Warren Mitchell. The writing team included Marty Feldman and Ronald Chesney.

Apart from radio, I also wrote intimate revue, summer shows, and many pantomimes for Beryl Reid and Ken Dodd. In 1959 I worked with Rodgers and Hammerstein on their version of *Cinderella* at the London Coliseum starring Tommy Steele.

In 1960 I decided to concentrate on television.

Most of the following credits are in collaboration with Ronald Chesney.

1961–1965	*The Rag Trade*	(Peter Jones/Mirian Karlin)	
1964–1967	*Meet the Wife*	(Thora Hird)	BBC
1966–1968	*Bedsit Girl*	(Sheila Hancock/Derek Nimmo)	
1970–1974	*On the Buses*		London Weekend Television
1970–1973	Co-Producer/Writer of full length features:		
	On the Buses; Mutiny on the Buses;		
	Holiday on the Buses		EMI-MGM
1974–1975	*Lotsa Luck*	(Dom DeLuise)	
		Directed by Carl Reiner	NBC, USA
1975	*Romany Jones*	(James Beck)	
		London Weekend Television	
1976	*Andre Van Duin Show*	Holland	

1975–77	*Don't Drink the Water*	London Weekend Televison
1977	*The Rag Trade*	(Peter Jones/Mirian Karlin)
	(New series)	London Weekend Television
1981	*Take a Letter, Mr Jones*	(John Inman/Rula Lenska)
		Southern TV
1983	*A Little Bit on the Side*:	An Yvonne Arnaud Theatre
	A revue for Beryl Reid	Guildford production. Other writers included Harold Pinter and Victoria Wood. Sixteen-week tour
1984	TV Festival at Banff, Canada (panellist, writers' workshop)	
1986	TV Festival at Banff, Canada Chairman of writers' workshop for the week of festival	
1987	*A New Life*	Stage comedy at the Queen Elizabeth Playhouse, Vancouver
1988	*A New Life*	Stage comedy at the New Century Theatre, Toronto
1988	*'Allo 'Allo*	(Two episodes only)
1989–94	*The Rag Trade*	Remade by Scandinavian TV as *Fredericksson's Fabriks*
1992	Script Consultant	Alomo Productions
1993	Script Consultant	Mediabord Komedy Haus, Hamburg
1994	*Fredericksson's Fabriks – The Movie!*	Feature film based on the Scandinavian *Rag Trade*
1994	*The Rag Trade*	Remade by Belgian BRTN
1995	*The Rag Trade*	Remade in Portuguese by Multicena of Lisbon as *Trapos and Company*
(1985–96	Visiting Tutor in Writing Comedy, at City University, London)	
2000	*The Rag Trade*	Remade in Afrikaans by Penguin Films of Johannesburg

1999–2002 Visiting Tutor/Lecturer at British National Film and TV School; British Film Institute Writing Workshops; Carlton TV (UK) New Writers' Sitcom Workshop; University of Barcelona; London Department of New York University; University of Kent School of Drama, Film and Visual Arts; Writers' Summer School, Swanwick; Sitcom Jury, Rose d'or TV Festival, Montreux

1   Getting started

Can you really teach anyone to write comedy?
No – the spark has to be there. Whilst the very best writing cannot be taught, much writing, especially new writing, even if it's mediocre, or even terrible, can be improved.

Is the layout of a script important?
Too many new writers waste too much time worrying about the layout, agonizing about whether the names of the characters should go in the centre of the page, like this:

HUSBAND:
(TIRED AND WEARY)
Darling, I'm home from work . . .

or at the side of the page, like this:

HUSBAND: (TIRED AND WEARY) Darling, I'm home from work . . .

or like this:

HUSBAND: Darling, (TIRED AND WEARY) I'm home from work . . .

Don't worry whether to put instructions in capitals or italics, or about the width of the margin. Don't waste time agonizing about technical terms; cuts – fade – close-up, etc.
  A good script is never rejected because of layout or lack of technical jargon. If people like it, then any experienced film

or television PA or secretary can lay it out in a professional manner and add all the technical terms necessary.

In the beginning, a script should be written so that it can be understood – that's all. Just stop worrying about the layout and write it! Finish it!

Many good scripts are not sold, not because of their layout, but because they haven't been finished.

*Are there different techniques when writing for
television, film, stage and radio?*
Yes – and these guidelines should help:

Put yourself in the place of the audience. Imagine you're one of the audience.

TELEVISION
This is usually watched by two or three people indoors in a living-room. Picture yourself sitting in front of the screen looking at the set.

Write and describe what you want to see on that screen, and what you want the characters to do and say.

Remember that the TV screen is small; a person full-length is reduced to about a fifth or a sixth of their actual size. Only the face can come out at roughly the right size. That's why television is very much a medium of close-ups.

FILMS
Again, imagine yourself in the audience at the cinema. When you're writing, visualize what you want to see on that screen. Television usually reduces everything; the cinema enlarges them . . . or blows them up to about forty or fifty times their size.

This explains why television comedy often has many scenes with just two or three people, or a family in a living-room, or an office. In films, this can be dreary – one needs to go for bigger scenes – more people – bigger visuals.

THE STAGE
Put yourself in a theatre – say halfway down the stalls, and think of what you want to see on the stage. The obvious difference from television and films is that there aren't any

close-ups; there aren't any cameras to pinpoint the gags and bits of business.

A gag, say, that relied on a suspicious wife finding strange lipstick on her husband's face would work on television or films, but would hardly be seen on the stage.

RADIO

Once more, think of what you want to hear – what you want to convey to your listener. Obviously no pictures – nothing visual. Use voices – sound effects – music – to create a mental picture in your listener's mind. If you want to set your scene in Victoria Station, have a sound effect on which listeners can hear background station noise and a train announcement. You can then have one of your characters saying: 'Victoria's more crowded than ever these days.' That's it. You've set the scene.

These are just the guidelines, and we'll go into more details later.

But first let's look at some gags and sketches:
Whatever your ultimate aim, writing gags and sketches is a useful experience, and in the States it is recognized as the normal way to embark on a comedy career.

Many of the top writers, such as Woody Allen, Neil Simon and Carl Reiner started this way. Top British writers have also followed the same route. Ray Galton and Alan Simpson wrote sketches for many radio shows before going on to *Hancock* and *Steptoe*.

Ray Galton:

> Writing sketches makes you very conscious of laughter. You find out what works, and what doesn't work. It helps you when you go on to write the half-hour sitcom. You make quite sure that you have some definite laughs as you go along.

Brian Cooke and Johnny Mortimer are creators and writers of many top rating sitcoms. One of their many successful shows was *Man About the House* which was adapted for the Americans as *Three's Company* and was top of the ratings in the States for many years. They started out writing sketches for radio.

Brian Cooke:

> After Johnny and I had finished a script we went through a process we called 'ticking the laughs'. We sat down with our producer, went through the script and ticked off lines which we reckoned should get a laugh. We liked to see three or four ticks on each page, that is, every third or fourth line. Because in radio, if you're not getting laughs, you're not getting anything.
>
> When we started writing for television we always did 'ticking the laughs', and if there weren't enough ticks on a page we'd do something about it. I don't mean that we would stick in an obvious gag, but we would strengthen the lines in the situation or maybe trim or tighten up some plot lines.

Andy Hamilton, who with Guy Jenkin, wrote and co-produced *Drop the Dead Donkey*, started out by writing gags and sketches.

Andy:

> In my first two years in the business I wrote mainly for radio – for *Weekending* and *Roy Huddlines*. Then when John Lloyd, my radio producer, left for television, I started in TV. I wrote for Marti Caine, Mike Yarwood . . . and I did a lot of work on *Not the Nine O'Clock News*. Sketch writing is valuable when you go to writing sitcoms. It stops you being boring because sketches are about compression. And they are also about taking an idea and developing it in a funny and interesting way. It's all about doing it economically. That's the positive side. Those years of sketch writing made me strict on my own stuff and taught me the value of rewriting.
>
> Sketch writing is valuable. The only downside is that you develop what I call the 'sketch writer's tic' – leaving funny lines in just because you like the sound of them rather than looking at a scene and saying, 'well actually, that line doesn't belong'. It takes you a while to get rid of that habit. But I have found that gradually, as I've got older, I am more grateful to the sketch writer's discipline than I first realized. When a script has gone well and people have liked it, I think, 'well, that's the sketch training coming through'.

2   *Are there any formulas?*

The full-length comedy script can be regarded as a skilful blend of gags and one-liners, sketches and routines, based on a strong storyline.

FORMULAS? Well, there are certainly some 'tricks-of-the-trade' which writers find useful.

Here's a gag that comics often use in a routine about marriage:

> My wife and I have talked about divorce, but it's the children that have kept us together. I didn't want them and she didn't want them!

or about schooldays:

> When I was in the sixth grade I was madly in love with my teacher. Trouble was, the difference in our ages. I was twenty-three and she was nineteen.

These are both reversal gags – the reversal of what normally happens . . . the unexpected impact that gets the laugh. (Don't ask me why. I think I know what gets laughs. I don't know why. Who does?)

THE REVERSAL is a useful tool when sketch-writing. Here's a sketch of mine about football pools:

> THE SETTING IS THE FRONT DOOR OF A SEMI-DETACHED. THE MAN FROM LITTLEWOODS, WITH A REPORTER, IS BREAKING THE NEWS TO A WORKING-CLASS COUPLE.

> MAN: Good morning, I'm from Littlewoods. On last
>   Saturday's Treble Chance only three people

15

won the top prize, and one million, four
hundred and fifty-eight thousand, two hundred
and seventy-six people lost. And I have great
pleasure in informing you that you are one of
those who lost.

HUSBAND: (BERSERK WITH JOY, HUGS HIS WIFE)
We've lost the pools, darling! We've lost! We've
lost!

WIFE: (OVERCOME WITH HAPPINESS)
It's luck! (WIPING AWAY TEARS OF JOY) We
know nothing about football . . . just picked
out the teams with a pin!

REPORTER: Is it going to make any difference to your way
of life?

HUSBAND: Oh, no. I won't let it go to my head, I'll carry on
just as though nothing has happened.

REPORTER: And do you think you'll be troubled by begging
letters?

HUSBAND: Oh, no, we'll go on sending them just the
same! . . .

And so the sketch carried on . . . a complete reversal.

There is a brilliant example of a reversal sketch in the
Monty Python film *The Meaning of Life*.

John Cleese – as a schoolmaster – is giving his form a
sex-lesson, with the help of his wife. They strip off to give a
practical demonstration of the sex act to the class. The
class-room of boys hardly glance at them. Absolutely bored,
they stare out of the window, read sporting and football
magazines behind their desks, and totally ignore the master
and his wife having sex on the desks in front of them.

This of course was the complete reverse of what boys
normally do, reading their sex books and porn magazines
surreptitiously during a boring lesson.

THE REVERSAL is also very useful for the very short sketch or
quickie – like this:

THE SET IS THE INTERIOR OF A LIVING-ROOM FEATURING THE
FRONT DOOR TO THE HOUSE OR APARTMENT.
THE MOTHER ANSWERS THE DOOR CHIMES.

THE DOOR OPENS TO REVEAL A VERY LARGE DOG AND A SMALL CHILD.

MOTHER: Oh, another stray! How many times do I have to tell you? You cannot keep bringing them home to this house. They're so messy indoors. Come along this minute!

SHE TAKES THE DOG'S LEAD, BRINGS THE DOG INSIDE AND CLOSES THE DOOR ON THE CHILD.

THE COMPARISON is a good way to get a laugh . . . comparing someone to something that's amusing, ridiculous, repulsive, bizarre. You might say about a girl who's a bit of a mess – 'She looks like an unmade bed' or 'She looks like a parcel done up ugly', or, 'Is she fat and ugly? From the front she looks like an elephant from the back!'

The comparison or looks like gag seems to be very useful when one woman is being bitchy about another.

A favourite of Beryl Reid's was when she was doing a routine, knocking her girlfriend Deirdre:

'Deirdre says her complexion is sallow . . . I call it yellow . . . what with her yellow face and her little black eyes, she looks like a small portion of prunes and custard!'

This gag always got a laugh whenever Beryl used it, but it wouldn't have worked with 'apricots and custard'. Prunes is a funny word – apricots isn't.

Some words are funny – some are not

Take this gag. A comic, talking about his tough upbringing, says:

The books in our local library were always greasy . . . in our district we used kipper bones as bookmarks!

This gag wouldn't have worked with haddock bones or plaice bones.

Be aware of words. Use words that will make an impact. Alliteration also helps. In a recent sitcom, a wife, suspecting her husband of having an affair said: 'I bet he's bonking some bimbo in the back seat!'

This is more expressive and funnier than saying: 'He's having sex with some girl in the rear of the car.'

EXAGGERATION – or, as some comics call them, the 'so much' gags

The talkative woman: 'She talks so much, when she sits on the beach her tongue gets sunburnt.'

The girl who likes her food: 'Does she eat! She eats so fast she gets sparks out of a knife and fork.'

OR

'If she goes more than twenty minutes without eating, she thinks she's got anorexia.'

The guy who likes his drink: 'After the last party they needed block and tackle to get out the empties.'

OR

'I met him on New Year's Eve – he was staggering around. I said: "Did you have a nice Christmas?" He said: "Yes, and I've still got Boxing Day to come." '

The untidy teenager: I said: 'You keep losing things. Where's your cheque book?' He said: 'In the salad bowl under my trainers.'

OR

'You should see his room. I said, "I don't expect you to clean it regularly, but at least every few months go in and rotate the crops".'

Without getting too analytical, a gag is often another way of saying something – a smart way – an exaggerated way to make the point.

EXAGGERATION can be useful in triggering the idea for a sketch.

Here is the outline of a sketch which is based on

exaggerating a very common worry about medicines and their side-effects:

> A highly-strung woman is about to go out. She took an aspirin for her headache – read the label about possible side-effects which warned about stomach irritations, etc. She took the stomach pill – the warning on the bottle said: 'May cause amongst other things blurred vision, excitement or restlessness'. So she took a valium to calm herself down. She read the side-effects of that which said: 'May cause nausea or unsteadiness', so she took a seasick tablet.

The sketch continued with her gulping down one pill after another; then she dashed off to her appointment. She didn't want to be late. And where was she going? To her doctor!

SWITCHING

One way of switching is to take a stereotyped, well-defined character and switch him/her from their usual and familiar setting to a different one to see how they behave.

There was an example of this during a strike by ambulance workers, and the army was called in. A sketch going the rounds at that time had the typical bullying Army Sergeant-Major dealing with the civilian casualties, bellowing at them:

> Come along, you dozy lot! Let's have you! All those with broken legs march smartly off to the fracture unit. Left, right, left right. That man there! Who gave you permission to groan? Stop it! That man – at the end there. Tuck that bone in! Looks most untidy protruding out of your leg! What a scruffy lot!
>
> etc . . . etc . . .

Another example of the professional man in a different setting. In this radio sketch, the surgeon and his nurse are at home, doing the washing up:

SURGEON: Saucepan . . .
NURSE: Saucepan . . .
SURGEON: Wire wool . . .
NURSE: Wire wool . . .
SURGEON: Brillo pad . . .

NURSE: Brillo pad . . .
SURGEON: Wine glass . . .
NURSE: Wine glass . . .
SURGEON: Oops!
NURSE: Oops!

FX: THERE IS A CRASH OF GLASS:

SURGEON: Dustpan . . .
NURSE: Brush!

ANOTHER TYPE OF SWITCHING IS ROLE-REVERSAL
This gives comedy from adults behaving like children, children like adults, humans like animals, animals like humans. There was a good example of this in a send-up of David Attenborough.

David Attenborough, of course, is often seen squinting through his binoculars at animals and creatures of the planet, and describing their habits in the greatest detail.

In the role-reversal sketch there were two frogs hidden outside Attenborough's house. With the usual binoculars, night glasses, infra-red cameras and ultra-sensitive microphones, they were spying on the Attenboroughs and describing the most intimate details of their private lives and mating habits, just as David might describe them.

Role-reversal is very much a standard device, not just for sketches but in plays and films. There have been so many comedies based on role-reversal, more commonly ones where men have to pretend to be women.

There's the evergreen *Charlie's aunt*. The film *Some Like It Hot* with Jack Lemmon and Tony Curtis disguised as a couple of girls in an all-girl orchestra to escape from gangsters. And *Tootsie* with Dustin Hoffman as an 'actress' in order to get work, and, more recently, *Nuns on the Run*, with crooks hiding in a nunnery.

THE SURPRISE
Surprising the audience can be a good way to get a laugh. You lead the audience along a certain path, you get them

thinking that something quite normal is happening – then WHAM! You surprise them:
Example:

TWO SKINHEAD TYPES IN A LIVING ROOM WATCHING TV AND OBVIOUSLY ENJOYING THE PROGRAMME. THE SHOW FINISHES AND THEY SWITCH OFF THE SET:

SKINHEAD: Right – that's it. Let's get back to work.

THEY BOTH PUT ON BURGLARS' MASKS, UNPLUG THE SET AND SNEAK OUT WITH IT.

Another classic example of the surprise was a Tracey Ullman sketch in the TV series *Three of a Kind*.

The sketch opened with a close-up of Tracey's face. She seemed to be lying down and in great agony, through all the cliché motions of a woman giving birth.
   Her perspiring face was being dabbed. She was being told to 'Push! Push! Push harder! Nearly there! A bit more! That's it!'

The camera then cuts to a full-length to show that Tracey was straining and struggling and pushing to get into a pair of tight jeans!

The surprise works well when writing one-liners. It's pretty simple when you get the hang of it. You make a statement, build up a picture, then knock it down.
   Example:

The comic introducing the band: 'They are a terrific bunch of musicians. Last night they played like they never played before – in tune!'

Introducing one of the acts: 'He really is a most generous man. Last night outside the hotel, I saw him give twenty pounds to a tramp. Actually she wanted twenty-five, but he beat her down.'

GOING FORWARD IN TIME

This trick usually works best by taking a broad topic of the day – say 'The Greenhouse Effect', the sea-level rising – and then going forward in time about fifty years, and exaggerating what might happen.

There's a good idea for a sketch showing the average family living under water, catching the submarine to work, and then in the evening taking the fish for a walk, etc etc.

GOING BACKWARDS IN TIME

Again, take a broad topic like, say, immigration and the way the British moan about foreigners. Taking this theme, go backwards in time almost a couple of thousand years to the time of the Roman invasion, and there's the basis for a sketch with two Britons moaning and groaning about the Romans pouring into the country, complaining that those foreigners shouldn't be allowed in – not unless they can play cricket!

They'd also complain about the Romans building their roads everywhere, destroying the countryside, just as people nowadays complain about the motorways:

'Their roads are destroying the environment.'
'I mean, who wants to march from London to Colchester in only four days.'

RECAP

While there are no formulas, these hints for gags and sketches should give you a start:

Reversals
Exaggerations
Comparisons
Switching
Role reversals
Surprise
Forwards in time
Backwards in time

3 How do you start to write a sketch?

Where do the ideas come from?
Well there is, of course, what is called 'divine inspiration', that brilliant idea that seems to come from nowhere. The trouble is they don't seem to come that often, so that the best thing is to sit down and beaver away.

The process goes like this:
Pick a subject – Is there a topic?
Very often there is something in the news that can spark you off. It is best to choose what I call a broad topic – not one that will only be a hot topic for a few days,but one that keeps cropping up like unemployment, inflation, fighting in the various flashpoints around the world.

I had to write a sketch for radio. For some reason I started thinking about Kate Adie, the famous BBC foreign correspondent, and came up with the following idea:

CONTINUITY: BBC foreign correspondents have a hectic time reporting back from the battle-torn hot spots; to give them a brief respite they are now being sent to report back from slightly different venues.

Over now to the Hammersmith Palais for *Come Dancing*, introduced this week by KATE ADIE.

MUSIC AND BACKGROUND UNDER TO SUIT DIALOGUE:

KATE: This is Kate Adie from the Palais of Hammersmith. I have just arrived, I have flown in non-stop from Shepherd's Bush. The atmosphere is tense, I can see couples who appear to be skirmishing . . . Oh!!

FX:

> BULLET WHINES PAST
> I had to duck quickly to avoid a flying sequin . . . Right in front of me there is a girl violently contorting in this atmosphere, something has to snap.

FX:

> SHORT CLOTH TEAR
> There goes her shoulder strap . . . Now I think her bra is going . . . it can't hold.
> Yes, her bra has gone and the police have their hands full.

The sketch continued along those lines . . .

A SKETCH IS ONE IDEA:
Barry Cryer (script editor – *The Russ Abbot Show*), who also writes many sketches with Peter Vincent:

> That one idea, that's all you need. One day Peter Vincent said: 'The rooftop restaurant on top of the Tower of Pisa.'
> I said, 'We're off and running'. As soon as you hear an idea like that you know you've got a sketch. If you don't you shouldn't be doing it. You're not a comedy writer.

That sketch was, of course, hilarious . . . Russ Abbot as the waiter trying to serve the dinner with everything sliding off the table on to the floor and the diners' laps.

ONE IDEA – BUT THERE ARE SOME ODD WAYS OF GETTING IT:
Barry Cryer recalls:

> One day I sat down with David Nobbs to write a sketch for Les Dawson.
> We were absolutely stuck. We just sat there drinking coffee after coffee.
> Then I had a mad idea. I said: 'Let's take that dictionary from the shelf and stick in a pin.'
> We opened it on one of the 'O' pages. The first word was ostrich. We made a decision . . . let's go with ostrich and see what happens.

The process went like this:

Les Dawson would not have an ostrich, but what would he have? A pigeon. How about if he entered an ostrich for a pigeon-breeders' race.

This led to Les having an argument with the organizers, Les insisted the race was for pigeon-breeders, not pigeons. He, as a pigeon-breeder, was entitled to enter an ostrich, and he had brought his ostrich with him. The ostrich was an actor in a skin. Actually, the actor was Roy Barraclough, of *Coronation Street*. Roy made a marvellous ostrich – squatting in the skin, with one arm raised up inside the neck.'

Ian Davidson (script editor), who also wrote some of the sketches for *The Two Ronnies*:

'A good trick in sketch writing is to think of what normally happens and stand it on its head.'

In other words, the **reversal**.

YOU HAVE TO START SOMEWHERE – PICK A SUBJECT
Say, for example, the subject you pick is PUBS AND DRINKING.

Let your mind revolve around the subject.
Look at it from one angle then another.
Is there a new angle?
What is happening in pubs at the moment (exaggerate those trends)
Visualize what normally happens.
Let's assume you try the **reversal** approach.

This was probably the type of process that led to a sketch in *The Two Ronnies*, based on the current fad for bottled water.

Corbett and Barker were in a pub tasting all the different brands of bottled water – Evian, Perrier, Welsh, Highland, Malvern, etc ... sipping them, rolling them round their mouths in the manner of two wine connoisseurs tasting wines. Sipping waters, rolling them round their tongues, then spitting them out. And the pay-off was the glasses being washed up in beer!

Keeping on the subject of pubs, add visualizing what normally happens. Now if two old friends meet in a pub, they insist on treating each other. Let's switch this custom to another setting – when they meet at the petrol station.

SET: TWO CARS AT A PETROL STATION:

NIGEL:	(TO ATTENDANT) Six gallons please. (TURNS AND SEES FRIEND) Roger! Well I never! Haven't seen you in ages. What are you going to have, old boy? A couple of gallons?
ROGER:	No thanks, old man, really.
NIGEL:	Oh, come along, I insist. (TO ATTENDANT) Miss, put another couple in my friend's car, will you?
ROGER:	No, no, please, old man. I've been filling up all morning. I've got a real tankful – just couldn't take another drop of petrol.
NIGEL:	Then have some oil?
ROGER:	No, old man, please . . .
NIGEL:	Go on, you haven't had one with me for a long time.
ROGER:	Well, all right then, just a pint.
NIGEL:	Miss, put a pint of oil in my friend's car please. How about you, Miss? Have you got a car here?
ATTEND.:	Yes, sir.
NIGEL:	Then have something yourself.
ATTEND.:	That's very kind of you, sir. I'll just have a spot of air in my tyres if you don't mind.
NIGEL:	Now let's have one for the road. Roger, do you know what's a good pick-me-up? A dash of distilled water for your battery.
ROGER:	(HESITANT) Well . . .
NIGEL:	Oh, go on . . . be a devil.
ROGER:	No, old boy. You just get one for yourself. But definitely no more for me. I'm driving!

When sketch-writing, nothing is better than an enquiring mind. Curiosity. What would happen if? How do they go about that? What's the angle? What's the slant?

PICK A TOPIC AND LET THE MIND WANDER ROUND IT:
A few years ago I had to write a sketch for Beryl Reid. A topic of the day was the Channel Tunnel. I started thinking

'tunnels' and wondered, 'How on earth does one set about buying a tunnel?' And I came up with this sketch which was for Beryl Reid playing one of her eccentric old ladies.

SET: A SECTION OF A HIGH-CLASS HARROD'S-TYPE STORE
BERYL ENTERS. SHE IMPATIENTLY BANGS THE SHOP BELL ON THE DESK. SALESMAN ENTERS – IN BLACK JACKET, STRIPED TROUSERS, A REFINED, DISCREET HARRODS/CARTIER TYPE:

SALES.: Good morning, madam. Can I help you?

BERYL: (WITH SMILE, AS THOUGH IT IS THE MOST NORMAL REQUEST IN THE WORLD)
I'd like to buy a tunnel.

SALES.: A tunnel? Yes . . . (REFERRING TO CATALOGUES, ETC, AS NECESSARY) Here we are. Now, what length of tunnel did you have in mind? How long?

BERYL: (FUMBLES IN HANDBAG, BRINGS OUT SOME NOTES. LOOSELY WOUND AROUND THEM IS AN ORDINARY TAPE MEASURE)
Let me see . . . I measured up this morning. Here we are . . . twenty-three miles. Well, actually not quite twenty-three, but one must allow for shrinkage. How much are they these days?

SALES.: They work out at two million pounds and ninety-nine pence per yard.

BERYL: Good Heavens! They've gone up since last time. Er – have you got any second-hand tunnels? Anything that's shop-soiled? Any remnants?

SALES.: No, madam, I'm sorry.

BERYL: (SARCASTICALLY) Of course not. I suppose you're keeping them for the January sales! Oh well, I'll settle for a new one . . . and it had better be good. If it's full of leaks, it'll come right back!

SALES.: Don't worry, madam. Now, is there anything else in this department while you're here? Bridges? Aquaducts? Canals? Dry docks? Lighthouses?

BERYL: No – I stocked up on those last time.

SALES.: Are you all right for submarines?

BERYL: Of course I am. How do you think I got here? Just the tunnel, that's all. I can't stand pushy salesmen. Just the tunnel. Can you deliver?

SALES.: But of course, madam. You are in our area. (CONSULTING BOOK) Let me see. Yes, we can deliver in about sixteen years' time.

BERYL: As quick as that? I don't want them to rush it.

SALES.: Oh, no . . . it will be fully guaranteed. Shall we say, then, that we'll deliver August the eighth, 2009?

BERYL: Morning or afternoon? I can't wait in all day.

SALES.: I'll make a note. Now, madam, are you quite certain there isn't anything else?

BERYL CONSULTS HER SHOPPING LIST.

SALES.: (CONTD) Oil rigs? Airships? Nuclear reactors?

BERYL: (CONSULTING LIST) Yes – a garlic crusher!

SALES.: (COMPLETELY THROWN) Oh dear! Oh dear! A garlic crusher! Now that is tricky. I suggest that Madam tries the basement . . . they handle the big stuff down there. Just the tunnel then?

BERYL: Yes.

SALES.: (WORKING OUT THE BILL) That'll be twenty-three miles at two million and ninety-nine pence a yard . . . That's eighty billion, nine hundred and sixty million, four thousand and seventy-five pounds, twenty pence.

BERYL: (PRODUCING CARD) American Express?

SALES.: Thank you . . . that will do nicely!

RECAP

We've talked about reversals, exaggerations, comparisons, switching, role reversals, surprise, going forward in time, and going backwards in time.

But the 'buying the tunnel' sketch didn't fall into any of these categories. Most sketches don't; they are a mixture – a bit of this and a bit of that. A combination.

Example: The Greenhouse effect sketch idea is a mixture – a combination of going forwards in time, plus exaggeration.

There are no rules in writing. What we've talked about are certain tricks of the trade. Think of them as 'tools' to start you off, to give you a spark. Then, with a lot of thinking, hard work and that necessary bit of talent, you should be able to produce some original work of your own.

4 The half-hour situation comedy

What is a situation comedy?
It is not a half-hour of one-liners and gags strung together. The laughs should come from the situation and the way the characters behave in that situation.

As we see in this extract of 'The Blood Donor' by Galton and Simpson, with Tony Hancock:

THE NURSE LEADS TONY INTO AN ANNEXE WHERE THE DOCTOR IS SITTING AT A TABLE. NEXT TO HIM ARE ALL THE PARAPHERNALIA REQUIRED FOR BLOOD DONATIONS.

DOCTOR: May I have your card please?
TONY: By all means. (HE SITS DOWN AND HANDS HIS CARD TO THE DOCTOR) I'm ready when you are, squire.
THE DOCTOR LOOKS AT THE CARD.
DOCTOR: Good. Hold your hand out, please.
TONY HOLDS HIS HAND OUT. THE DOCTOR CLEANS TONY'S THUMB AND THEN PICKS UP THE NEEDLE.
DOCTOR: Now this won't hurt. You'll just feel a slight prick at the end of your thumb.
TONY WINCES IN READINESS, SCREWING HIS EYES SHUT.
CUT TO DOCTOR AS HE JABS THE NEEDLE IN.
TONY WINCES AGAIN, THEN HAS A LOOK AT THE END OF HIS THUMB. HE BEAMS PROUDLY.
TONY: Dear oh dear. Well that's that. I'll have my cup of tea and my biscuit now. Nothing to it, is there really. I can't understand why everybody doesn't do it. (GETS UP) Well, I'll bid you

good-day, thank you very much, whenever you
want some more, don't hesitate to get in touch
with me.

DOCTOR: Where are you going?

TONY: To have my tea and biscuits.

DOCTOR: I thought you came here to give some of your
blood?

TONY: You've just had it.

DOCTOR: That was just a smear.

TONY: It may be just a smear to you, mate, but it's life
and death to some poor wretch.

DOCTOR: No, no, no. I've just taken a small sample to
test.

TONY: A sample? How much do you want then?

DOCTOR: Well, a pint of course.

TONY: A pint? have you gone raving mad? Oh well, of
course . . . I mean, you must be joking.

DOCTOR: A pint is a perfectly normal quantity to take.

TONY: You don't seriously expect me to believe that. I
mean, I came here in all good faith to help my
country. I don't mind giving a reasonable
amount, but a pint . . . why, that's very nearly
an armful. I'm sorry, I'm not walking around
with an empty arm for anybody . . .

There was laugh after laugh in that sequence, with some of
the biggest laughs coming on lines like:

'Well, I'll bid you good-day, whenever you want any more,
don't hesitate to get in touch with me.'
AND
'To have my tea and biscuits.'

Such lines are very, very funny when said by *that* character
in *that* situation, but of course they mean absolutely nothing
out of context.

It's the characters that count

A normal person going to give blood is not funny, but when
Hancock became a blood donor it became a comedy classic.
The situation was real and normal, the character wasn't.
Danny Simon (doyen of American scriptwriters – his

brother Neil Simon and Woody Allen started their careers
working for him and learnt their craft under his guidance):

> Situation comedy should really be called 'character comedy'.
> The laughs come from the reaction of your characters to that
> situation . . . When you are writing, your characters are your
> collaborators.

Construction

The *Hancock Half Hours* were a vehicle designed to exploit
the talents of one star, but most sitcoms such as *Yes Minister,
To the Manor Born, Only Fools and Horses, Cheers, The
Golden Girls*, etc. feature a small group of characters.

How are they constructed?

Each half-hour episode can be regarded as something like
the last two acts of a traditional three-act play in that the
characters and setting are already known to the audience.

Not only are the characters known, but also their
relationships and attitudes to each other.

If we switch on *Yes Prime Minister* and see Sir Humphrey
and secretary doing a bit of crafty plotting, we know almost
certainly that it is the Prime Minister they're plotting against.

In TV comedy you have to grab your audience quickly. If
it's a comedy they'll expect some laughs in the first minute or
two, or they'll switch off or change channels. They want
laughs, not loads of explanatory dialogue and plot.

And that's possible because *in an established series* the
audience already know what I call 'Act One'; the setting, the
characters, their relationships and attitudes. In fact, all the
necessary background information.

Starting a new series

The audience doesn't know the set-up. Information has to be
got across as quickly as possible to avoid the load of
explanatory dialogue. But there are tricks which experienced
writers use quite often.

Let's look at some successful shows: *M*A*S*H . . . Porridge
. . . Dad's Army . . . Bilko . . . On the Buses . . . 'Allo 'Allo
. . . Hi-de-Hi.*

These all have a common factor . . . a link – **Uniforms**.

Most of the characters in these shows are in some kind of uniform. Uniforms are a marvellous device when writing.

When the show starts, even in the very first episode the audience know immediately who's who. The chain of command, the relationship and attitudes. You can get on with the comedy with the minimum of explanatory dialogue.

In *M*A*S*H*, *Bilko*, *Dad's Army*, *'Allo 'Allo*, most of the characters are in military uniform, and those that aren't are clearly defined by their dress, like the waitresses in *'Allo 'Allo*.

In *Porridge*, the series set in a prison, the officers are in uniform, the prisoners in a form of battle dress, and the governor in a suit. So, again, we know immediately who's who.

Uniforms can also tell you a lot about the individual character. In *On the Buses*, the moment you see someone like Reg Varney – a middle-aged cockney – in a bus driver's uniform, you know right away a good deal about him.

You know what he's earning, the sort of place he lives in, and what sort of life he leads.

Another advantage is that people in uniform are usually found in a well-defined, easily recognizable setting; an army camp; a prison.

The uniform is therefore a marvellous device to give our audience instant information.

ALL CLOTHES ARE A TYPE OF UNIFORM
The way your characters are dressed can tell your audience so much about them.

> An obvious example is *Steptoe and Son*. The moment you see Harold Steptoe and his dad with the flat cap, battered trilby, choker and shabby clothes, you have a good idea of their types. And then in the opening caption when you see them with their horse and cart, you already have a lot of information about the show before it has even started.

ACCENT
In *Yes Prime Minister*, Sir Humphrey might say: 'With respect Prime Minister, I venture to suggest, if I may, that one might find further briefing on this matter extremely useful.'

He doesn't say: 'Prime Minister, I fink you dan't not know nuffink abawt it.'

In England especially, you learn a great deal about a person the moment they start speaking: Accent, grammar, articulation, manner of speech are a giveaway to background, education and status.

OPENING THE SHOW WITH AN INTERVIEW

If you want your audience to know details about your characters, the interview is useful.

A few years ago, Ronald Chesney and I wrote a show for Southern TV – a role reversal idea with John Inman as the personal secretary to a top woman executive, Rula Lenska.

In the opening episode, we had a reporter coming to do a piece about her – on her personal and business problems. This enabled us to get across a great deal of information about the show.

Here are some excerpts from the first few pages:

SET:
RULA AND JOHN ARE IN A LUXURIOUS EXECUTIVE OFFICE

JOHN: . . . At two o'clock that reporter from the *Daily News* is coming to interview you.

RULA: Oh yes, it'll be the usual male chauvinist article, 'Can a woman really be a top executive?' He did one last week about a woman who's become a commercial airlines pilot. As if that's so extraordinary.

JOHN: Well, it's a bit unusual.

RULA: I don't see why. I'm sure if I set my mind to it I could fly a jumbo jet across the Atlantic and bring it down safely.

JOHN: Well . . . I don't know. I did notice that it took you twenty minutes this morning to reverse your car in to the car park.

RULA: A jumbo jet does not fly in reverse.

JOHN: No, well you haven't flown one yet.

RULA: (STARTS TO TIDY HER DESK.) Never mind that, a decision-maker's desk should always be clean . . . free from clutter.
            SHE TAKES A FRAMED PHOTOGRAPH OFF THE DESK.

RULA:	I think I'd better put away this photo of Lucy.
JOHN:	(LOOKING AT PHOTO) Oh, she's sweet.

WE SEE IT IS A PHOTOGRAPH OF RULA AFFEC-
TIONATELY CUDDLING A YOUNG GIRL OF ABOUT
SEVEN YEARS OLD.

RULA: (WARMLY) I know . . . But I don't want to appear too maternal. (SHE TAKES ANOTHER PHOTOGRAPH FROM THE DRAWER.) This is more impressive.

WE SEE IT IS A PHOTOGRAPH OF RULA IN EVENING
DRESS, HAPPILY HOLDING A GLASS OF
CHAMPAGNE.

RULA: I think I look quite good on that.

JOHN: (LOOKING AT INSCRIPTION ON PHOTO) You ought to, it was taken ten years ago! You do look happy. What were you celebrating? Your divorce?

RULA: Oh really. I could not be divorced ten years ago if my child is only seven! No pregnancy lasts over three years.

JOHN: Well, you are a bit of a ditherer . . . But I'll take your word for it.

RULA: That photo was to celebrate my first pro-motion. Woman of the Year.

THE REPORTER IS USHERED IN BY THE RECEP-
TIONIST. THERE ARE THE USUAL 'HELLO'S', THEN
RULA INTRODUCES JOHN.

RULA: This is my personal secretary.

REPORTER: A woman executive with a male secretary. I'll make a note of that . . . quite unusual.

RULA: I don't see why. In these days there's no longer any sex discrimination . . . I was chosen for this job from amongst ten men.

JOHN: Yes – and I was chosen for the job of secretary from amongst sixteen girls.

REPORTER: (TO RULA) There is one aspect of your job that intrigues me. I don't really see how a woman such as yourself could . . .

(LOOKING AT NOTES) I see you are now a single parent. How do you combine the jobs of executive and mother?

RULA: (BRISKLY – WITH SUPREME CONFIDENCE) Delega-
             tion and organization. I have a very efficient
             housekeeper. My domestic life is never allowed
             to intrude into the office.

Note: From that moment the story started. The housekeeper
         had arrived in the outer office with Rula's daughter
         who was screaming her head off, having a tantrum
         because she didn't want to go to the dentist. John
         Inman had to go and pacify and keep her away from
         the reporter, which triggered off our first comedy
         scene.

         If you look back over these few lines, you will see
         we told our audience that Rula was divorced, had a
         child and a housekeeper, and John Inman was her
         personal secretary – necessary information.

Once you start thinking about it, you will realize that there
are many ways to give your audience essential information
about your characters.

Interviews are obvious ones, but there are also job
applications . . . applying for a loan . . . social security . . . a
mortgage.

There's always a way. In fact, if you're ever going to be any
good as a writer, you'll find a way to establish your
characters and set the scene as quickly and crisply as possible.

There is no time in a sitcom in comedy for extraneous
dialogue or padding. In the thirty-minute sitcom, the writer
doesn't even have thirty minutes. Deduct a minute and a half
for opening and closing captions, another two minutes for
laughs. That leaves just twenty-six minutes for the writer. But
that's on BBC. On ITV you have to deduct another three to
four minutes for the commercial break. This leaves just about
twenty-two minutes for the script.

Every word is precious, which is why, in comedy,
especially the sitcom, there are only three reasons for a line of
dialogue:

It should get a laugh, establish character, or further the
plot. A good line does all three.

If you think about all the sitcoms that have been done over
the years, most of them fall into roughly three basic types: the
VEHICLE FOR A STAR, such as Hancock, Roseanne, Bill

Cosby and Lenny Henry in *Chef*; the DOMESTIC, that is two, three or four people living under the same roof, such as husbands and wives, families, relatives, lodgers etc; and there is what I call THE GANG SHOW.

THE GANG SHOW features about eight regular characters who are found in the same setting each week, as in *Drop the Dead Donkey, Cheers*, etc.

The advantages are enormous for the writer – you don't have to worry about how to get your characters 'on' or 'off ', you don't have to worry about entrances and exits – your characters are there waiting to be used.

Think of the set-up in *Cheers* – there's the bar staff, Sam, Woody, Carla, and Rebecca the manageress, and the regulars, Frasier at the main counter, and Norm the fat guy always perched on his stool at the corner of the bar, and always next to Cliff the postman.

The writers can visualize them as they write, they can 'see' them in the set. This makes for a tighter script which needs less alterations or adjustments.

If the writer wants Carla, the waitress, to exchange a line or two with Norm, it's simple. We see Carla at the counter collecting some drinks, she takes them to a table *en route* for the dialogue with Norm, then continues on her way.

This type of sitcom can be very slick, very fast. You keep in the one basic set, it's the characters that move. You could say this type of show can be almost choreographed.

Another bonus is that in rehearsal the actors don't have to familiarize themselves with a new set which they may not see until the day of the recording. The director does not have to worry about where to place his actors, they automatically go to the same 'positions' each week.

One of the advantages of starting a gang show with eight regular characters is that you have what I call eight 'insurance policies' against failure. If only five of the characters work you would still have a reasonable show, if they all work then, as in *Cheers* and *Donkey*, you have a hit.

Another point to consider is what happens if there have to be cast changes – if for some reason a regular member has to leave. In a gang show it is easier to have a cast change, the residual team should be good enough to keep the show running while the new member fits in.

5 The writers' friend – What goes wrong?

When you sit down to write your comedy script, a good jumping off point is to have your characters set out to do something which is normally quite straightforward, then ask yourself, 'What goes wrong?'

When things go wrong there's conflict, problems, complications
Comedy should spring from the reaction of your characters to these circumstances.

If things did not go wrong there would be no problems, no comedy.

EXAMPLE: The film *Clockwise* written by Michael Frayn.

John Cleese is on his way to make an important speech, but 'What goes wrong?' He catches the wrong train. This one mistake leads to a hilarious chase across country, clashes with the police, suspected of abducting a schoolgirl, and Cleese even hitchhikes across Norfolk in a monk's habit.

If nothing went wrong, if he'd caught the right train, there would have been no problems, and no story.

A TOUCH OF KIPLING
Although you may start with 'What goes wrong' there are other details you need to help your script. You ask more questions.

Writing is so often asking question after question, or to quote Rudyard Kipling's favourite doggerel:

37

I keep six honest serving-men
(They taught me all I knew);
Their names are What and Why and When
And How and Where and Who

A step by step comedy sequence using 'What goes wrong?' and a touch of Kipling

A MAN'S TROUSERS NEED REPAIRING – THERE'S A TEAR IN THE BACK
What's the problem? If he's at home he has another pair, there's no problem.

WHERE IS HE?
Let's put him somewhere where he can't easily get help. Let's put him on the train.

WHY IS HE ON THE TRAIN?
He has a crucial business meeting, and he is being met at the station by some important clients. He has a deadline . . . a target. Just so much time to make the repair. This gives tension, conflict, chance of more things going wrong.

HOW IS HE GOING TO MAKE THE REPAIR?
In his briefcase he could have one of those little give-away sewing kits from a hotel. He could try and reach round and sew up the repair, perhaps in his panic he makes the tear worse.

HE IS NOW IN A PREDICAMENT. THE SEQUENCE COULD CONTINUE THIS WAY:
He goes to the toilet, takes off his trousers to repair them properly.
    Not very experienced at needlework, he's bending over, squinting.
    His contact lens falls out.
    He gets down on his hands and knees trying to find the lens. It slides under the door into the corridor.
    He opens the door to reach out for his lens.
    The train lurches, and goes through a tunnel – everything goes black.

When it's light again, our 'hero' is on hands and knees crawling down the corridor without his trousers.

IMMEDIATELY THERE ARE OTHER POSSIBILITIES:
He might be about to go back to the toilet to retrieve his trousers, when someone comes along, dashes into the toilet and slams the door.

While waiting for them to come out, he might duck into the next apartment. There's a girl there in a mini skirt who screams for the guard.
OR:
He could get back to his compartment, put on his raincoat, then wait outside the toilet. Then when the ticket collector comes along he opens his raincoat to get his ticket, exposes his bare legs and is accused of being a flasher! Maybe, when the train arrives, the important group of VIPs waiting to meet him are somewhat astonished to find him being escorted off the train and handed over to the police.

I think this demonstrates the comedy situations and possibilities that arise when you set out to achieve something quite simple, and then start asking questions beginning with 'What goes wrong?'

Can a comedy sequence be developed from any normal activity?
Usually it can.

Start with an everyday chore like shopping.

Where's the fun? Find the angle.

Shopping is too broad a topic. We have to narrow it down. We do this by asking ourselves questions . . .

Who goes shopping? What's special about them?

Let's decide that a Jewish man goes shopping because there are certain foods that Jews are not supposed to eat.

So our friend Goldberg is in the supermarket, he's sneaked in because he really fancies some bacon for his breakfast.

He selects a packet of bacon, there it is in his wire basket, and then, what happens? What goes wrong?

Well, it's pretty obvious. His rabbi comes in. Now right away we have a situation.

Goldberg could hide the bacon in his pocket, then, when he gets to the checkout, be accused of shoplifting.

OR:

He could hide the bacon in his newspaper. The rabbi asks to borrow the paper and goes off with it. He could be the one stopped at the checkout and accused of shoplifting.

OR:

The rabbi could go to the synagogue and it could fall out of his newspaper in his office in front of other people, much to his embarrassment. Maybe he spots it first and tries to hide it before other people can see it.

When things go wrong, things start to happen. We get problems, conflict, situations, in fact something to write about.

In this example, Goldberg was doing something that he shouldn't have been doing.

A tangled web

When our characters deliberately set out on some form of deception and things go wrong – there are even more problems.

Let's take a look at the following sequence:

A woman is in bed with her lover. It's mid-afternoon. What's the problem? How do we get some fun?

Take the obvious – the husband comes home unexpectedly. And immediately we're into a situation.

There are so many possibilities here, that we can understand why this premise is used so often in farce and comedies.

Let's consider some of them:

The wife could hide all evidence of her lover being there – clothing, cigarettes, drinks.

OR:

She could hide her lover in the bathroom. There could be fun trying to stop the husband from going to the hiding place.

OR:

She could pretend he's a repair man come to fix the plumbing or the electric wiring, which of course he can't do. When the husband is suspicious, the lover is forced to try and do the

'repair', causing chaos and confusion and flooding, or by fusing all the electric, nearly setting fire to the house.
OR:
The wife has to think up an excuse for being half-undressed in bed in mid-afternoon. She says she wasn't feeling well. A bit depressed, the husband might send for the doctor.

To cheer her up . . . the husband undresses and gets into bed with her. She is forced to make love with her husband while her lover sneaks out.
OR:
To really complicate matters, perhaps the husband has sneaked in with his secretary — thinking his wife would be out.

There are countless possibilities and permutations.
You can never go wrong if you start with 'What goes wrong?'

6 Writing a sitcom – Questions always asked

How long does it take to write an episode?
Most writers usually allow about two weeks. But if you're also currently in the throes of making the show, you are going to lose a couple of days writing time to go to read-throughs, rehearsals and recording in the studio. If you're lucky, you might manage the odd half-day off, so that leaves about ten to eleven days.

What's the first step in writing an episode?
Most successful writers would not think of starting until they have worked out the story line.

John Esmonde and Bob Larbey – creators and writers of *Please Sir, The Good Life, Ever Decreasing Circles*, etc:

> The story line is the hardest part. We spend at least half of our writing time on it. We find that if we've got our story line in great detail, we can sit back and enjoy it. It's more fun for us.
>
> We've learnt by bitter experience to write out our story line in great detail. When we started writing in the early days, we sometimes got to page 20, had another fifteen pages to write and found we were stuck, not knowing which way to go.

George Layton created and wrote the award-winning series *Don't Wait Up* starring Nigel Havers. This ran for thirty-nine episodes and won the Television and Radio Industries Club Award for Best Comedy of 1988. George is a writer who finds it essential to get his story line first:

I've never written gags or sketches. My first writing was a book of short stories, and then a TV play for drama.

In comedy, all my laughs come from the story, the twists and turns of the plot and the sub-plot. Before I start to write I must get the structure right. I must know where I'm going and how the story is going to end. Though, of course, when you do start writing you nearly always think of a better pay-off or an extra twist or two to the plot.

I appreciate that some writers don't work that way. I don't know, but I imagine that Carla Lane doesn't structure her scripts in great detail, but has the ability and that special talent to sit down and just write. I say this because I think her work is a 'stream of consciousness' . . . a segment of life. I only tried a couple of times to write a script, not knowing where I was going . . . just a vague idea . . . and quite frankly they tended not to be my best efforts.

The story line:

If necessary, be prepared to spend half of your writing time – say, up to five days – hammering out the story and making certain it will give you all the funny scenes you need. It's not wise to start writing until you're certain that your story line is strong enough and fruitful enough to sustain.

HOW DO I KNOW IF THE STORY LINE IS RIGHT?
You never really 'know', but a good test is to write down the story. In a half-hour episode, check that it has got at least five scenes or routines that should last five or six minutes each.

There is nothing worse than being halfway through writing the script, only to realize that the idea wasn't as fruitful as you thought, and you have run out of steam.

Do you go back to base and start on a different story line, or struggle on hopefully in a near-panic situation for a day or two? The deadline is looming up – your producer is on the phone – and you're stuck! This is torture! Believe me, this is something to be avoided!

How do you judge the length of a script? How many pages would there be in the average half-hour?
Don't go by the number of pages. The same script could be about thirty pages or fifty pages, depending on who types it, the spacing, the layout.

Never count the pages. A safer method is to count the number of speeches. I mean speeches, not lines of dialogue. I know that a speech might be just three or four words, or three or four lines – but it averages out. The average sitcom runs to about 350 speeches on BBC and about 300 on ITV. There were seventy-two episodes of *On the Buses* and each script ran to about 310 speeches, irrespective of the fact that some weeks there was much more 'business' than other weeks. I know it doesn't seem logical, but it's a fact. Counting the number of *speeches* is the best guide I know to the length of a script.

What do you do about the commercial break?

You've captured your audience, they're following the story and hopefully enjoying it, then wham! Three to four minutes of commercials.

The problem is that your show might be taking place in a normal working-class house, and when the adverts come on they're fast, trendy, glossy, often shot on location with bikini-clad models prancing around on sunlit tropical beaches. They're well-produced and expensive – it's possible for one commercial to cost as much as your half-hour sitcom. They are a distraction not to be ignored when plotting out your show.

If you want to hold your audience, you must write towards the commercial break, and make sure that the first half ends on a cliffhanger so that, although they may be watching the commercials, they haven't completely forgotten about the show.

The first minute or two after the commercial break is equally important. It's always best to reiterate the plot – remind them of the situation and try at the same time to get laughs – you have to hook your audience all over again.

What about the pay-offs?

The ideal pay-off should wrap up the story, solve everything with a big surprise, and at the same time get a big laugh. Unfortunately, these ideal pay-offs are not easy to come by, but before writing the script do have what I call a 'standby pay-off'. That is, a neat ending to your story. It may not be a fantastic surprise, it may not get a laugh, but it should wrap up your story in an acceptable way. At least it will be something to work towards. When you then start the actual writing and are immersed in your story, usually you have a flash of inspiration and think of something better. If you don't, then at least you will have an ending which will get you out of trouble.

IF YOU ARE HAPPY ABOUT YOUR STORY LINE YOU WILL WRITE YOUR SCRIPT WITH CONFIDENCE, YOU WILL BE MORE RELAXED IN A HAPPY FRAME OF MIND, AND THE FINAL RESULT WILL BE BETTER.

7 Hammering out the story line

Let's imagine that the story line is for a half-hour domestic sitcom. The aim is to have a beginning – a middle – and an end. About six funny scenes.

How do you know if a scene is funny?
If when you think of it you can almost immediately think of a couple of funny lines or a funny bit of business, it's quite likely when you write up that scene in full that it will be really funny.

But there are no guarantees – that's why you need a lot of ideas so that if one doesn't work out you can use another. Think of them as insurance policies.

Let's start the story line with this premise:
The young executive and his newly married wife are at home. It's Sunday night. A big night. The boss and his wife are coming to dinner for the first time.

What's the problem?
The wife is a lousy cook. She arranges for a haute cuisine, cordon bleu dinner to be delivered, almost ready to serve.

What goes wrong?
The wife gets a phone call to say that the delivery van has been involved in an accident and, while the husband is extolling her virtues as a cordon bleu cook, the actual haute cuisine four-course dinner is oozing down the hard shoulder of the M25.

What happens next? What are the possibilities?
Let's assume that the dinner is going to come, but will be very

late. The young executive and his wife have to stall their dinner guests for a couple of hours. How?

They could keep giving them drinks – maybe spike their drinks so that they get a bit drunk.

Get them involved in a game of trivial pursuits, a card game – something to really absorb them so that they don't notice the time.

The wife, after a few drinks and getting desperate, might suggest strip-poker.

The boss could be a bit of a dirty-old-man who fancies the wife, so she deliberately keeps losing, taking off more bits and pieces. When the dinner eventually arrives, she opens the door practically naked. The delivery man eyes her and says:

'What have you been up to then? Working up an appetite?'

OR:
Because of the accident, the dinner might not be coming at all. This could give a scene with the young wife in the kitchen frantically trying to whip up a meal from whatever is available.
OR:
Making some excuse to nip out to the nearest takeaway or helpful neighbour.

Have we got enough scenes?
Maybe not. We ought to get a couple more good scenes before, just to be on the safe side.

Try starting the story line earlier:
At the moment we start on Sunday night, just before the dinner guests arrive.

Supposing we start the night before – the Saturday night?

What might they be doing the night before?

Tarting up the house a bit. A DIY job – the husband slapping some paint around the downstairs loo.

The wife might have her hair in curlers while she's wearing some sort of face mask.

She could also be struggling into the dress she's going to wear the following night because it needs some kind of alteration.

Tomorrow night everything is to be lovely, but tonight it's chaos. The last thing they want tonight are visitors!

What happens? What goes wrong?
There is a phone call from the boss. He is speaking from his car to say they've been held up in the traffic; they will be a little late, but not to worry. They will be with them in less than an hour.

> PANIC! THEY SCREAM AT EACH OTHER. THERE'S BEEN A MIX-UP OVER THE DATE. THEY ARE COMING A DAY EARLY! GOD ALMIGHTY! THEY'LL BE HERE IN ONE HOUR'S TIME.

This, of course, leads to a frantic scene getting the house ready, the wife scraping off the face mask, the husband finishing painting the loo and getting dressed – ordering the meal to be delivered. (Because they've ordered so late, there could be more problems.)

How do we end our story? What are the possibilities?
Has the dinner been a success or not?

> There could have been one disaster after another, leading to the boss and his wife leaving in a huff.
> OR:
> There could have been a series of disasters which they've managed to cover up or explain away, and the dinner ends on a successful note.
> OR:
> There is one disaster after another, culminating in some catastrophe which they just can't explain away. They decide to make a clean breast of it – explain that they made a mistake about the date. They thought it was the Sunday instead of the Saturday, and apologize profusely.
>   The boss, far from being annoyed, is impressed, and says:

> You made a mistake, then moved heaven and earth to put it right and damned near got away with it. That's the sort of action I like in a young executive.
>   (SMILES ALL ROUND)
> OR:

If you think that it's unlikely that a young executive would make a mistake over such an important dinner date, then maybe the boss got the date wrong. Just when things are chaotic, the boss's wife looks in her diary, (WE'LL FIND A REASON) and discovers the mistake. The boss now realizes why the dinner has been so chaotic and congratulates the young executive as before.

If coming on the wrong day seems a bit contrived, is there another possibility?

Supposing it has been deliberately planned by the boss – the show could end something like this.

Things have gone terribly wrong. They've run out of excuses, they expect the boss to storm out at any moment, but he confesses:

'You must forgive us, but we deliberately came on the wrong night, just to see how you would deal with the situation. This is the test I often give to young executives and their wives when they join the firm. Quick thinking in a panic situation to see how they will react in a crisis.'

(SMILES ALL ROUND)

By starting the story earlier, we have gained another scene and some twists in the plot.

But there are some other tricks we could have tried to get an extra scene or two

1 **Finishing our story later, going to another setting**. Instead of finishing with the boss and his wife leaving after dinner, there could be a scene in the office the next day.
   OR:
   They could have drunk too much to drive home, so they have to stay the night.
2 **Bringing in another character**. When you are about three-quarters of the way through a show, the arrival of a new character can usually give impetus to the story, liven things up and give an extra scene.
   In the 'Boss to dinner' story line, the new character could be an unexpected visitor who is an embarrassment

– maybe a coarse, drunken friend or a relative. (There could be a situation keeping him/her away from the boss.)

In fact, anyone who is likely to cause problems – a hysterical next-door neighbour – an ex-lover, ex-wife/ husband, a debt collector, or someone to repossess the Porsche, etc, etc.

3   Insert a 'Fantasy' scene. Examples are:

THE FLASHBACK: In a short sequence, we could see the young wife, perhaps as a schoolgirl, cooking and burning everything.

THE DAYDREAM: The wife visualizes her worst fears. She poisons the dinner guests. They collapse at the table, their faces falling forward into their bowls of soup.
OR:
We could have a mad, crazy cooking scene – a speeded-up version of *Babette's Feast* – the wife dashing into the kitchen with live geese and turtles – then dashing out with the food all cooked.

These scenes can be effective and can get you out of trouble if you desperately need to liven up a script. But they must be kept short and sharp – they are more of an 'insert' than a scene which furthers the plot.

While the sitcom has been used as an example for this chapter, the same approach can be useful when working out the story line for a comedy feature film or stage play.

Most comedy writers don't like to start actually writing the script until they have a carefully constructed story line with many good scenes, and with each scene leading naturally to the next scene. They like to visualize the whole picture, to know what they're writing and where they are going.

However, there are some writers – probably just a few – who put paper in the typewriter and happily bash away, not quite sure where they're going, what the next scene is, or how the whole lot is going to end. But somehow it works out and they finish up with a fantastic script.

This approach is not to be recommended for beginners.

While there are a few writers who can do this, you might not be one of them.

RECAP – THE STORY LINE

The basic idea

After you have thought of the idea, can you – after say two or three hours working on it – be confident that it has at least two good comedy scenes? If not, don't bother. Think of something else – start working on another idea. Don't abandon ideas, put them on the back burner and sometimes – perhaps two or three months later – you will often find that you've got a new slant on them.

Ways of developing the idea

Start the story earlier. Usually good for at least one scene. And then what happens? Continue your original idea, again it should be good for at least one more scene.
Bring in a fresh character.
Go to another setting.
If desperate – is there a flashback or a fantasy scene?

8   *Visual comedy*

There is nothing like a good visual gag. When they work they're marvellous. They are remembered long after all the clever one-liners are forgotten.

One well-remembered visual was in the film *The Apartment.*

> Jack Lemmon was cooking some spaghetti. He wanted to strain it, couldn't find the strainer, so he picked up a tennis racket and strained the spaghetti through that. This was a big laugh in the cinema.

Using something for a totally different purpose . . . using it in an unexpected way surprises the audience and usually gets a big laugh – a surprise laugh.

In *On the Buses* we got some big laughs from the heater that Olive used for heating up her Carmen hair rollers:

This was the situation:

> Olive and Arthur were in a motel room. They had a Chinese takeaway that had got cold.
> Arthur was moaning.
> Olive got out her Carmen heater and plugged it in.
> Arthur: Good God! You are going to start curling your hair at this time of night.
> Olive: (PLEASED WITH HERSELF) No, I'm warming up the spring rolls.
> (SHE STARTED PUSHING THE SPRING ROLLS ON TO THE SPIKES.)

This worked well, and built into a nice little routine. Again, using some familiar item for a different purpose.

Another example of this type of visual was a routine of Michael Bentine – one of the original Goons:

Bentine had worked up a good comedy routine using a big sink plunger – the type that is a long wooden rod, like a short broomstick, with a black moulded rubber cup on the end. Bentine would fold up his leg and put his knee in the cup, and he was a one-legged sailor. He would put the cup on his head, and with the stick set at an angle, he would be a tram car or a trolley bus.

He had about twenty different ways of using that plunger, and with each variation he got a laugh.

There's a Chinese proverb: 'One picture is worth ten thousand words.'

When you have a tricky bit of plotting to do, or want to convey a mood, you can sometimes do this with a visual bit of business. Here are some examples:

1 In Carla Lane's *Butterflies*, Wendy Craig as Rhea, a frustrated bored housewife, is about to go out, hoping to meet a man who obviously fancies her. She is in a bit of a dither. Does she go out and get involved? Does she want to start an affair?

   She pauses in front of the mirror in the hall. She loosens the top of her dress, pulls down the neckline to show some more cleavage than usual. She beams at herself, pleased with the result. Then, a sudden tinge of guilt; she raises her neckline and is quite respectable again, then she hurries off.

That little bit of business in front of the mirror told us so much.

   Does she want to start an affair? Maybe she does. Maybe she doesn't. It's a tempting thought. But, oh no, she mustn't get involved ... it's all so ridiculous, but she's flattered by his attention and goes out to meet him anyway – in a bit of a dither.

This bit of business conveyed her feelings and, at the same time, there was a nice laugh when she hurriedly pulled up that neckline.

That's the way to do it. Think of a visual way to tell

something about a character, or to set the mood . . . then top
it with a laugh.

2 Desperately trying to keep young, we see a middle-aged man
somewhat overweight. He is jogging round the park, his
tracksuit and trainers brand new; he obviously doesn't jog
very often. He is puffing and panting, keeps lecherously ogling
the young attractive girls who are also out jogging.

This establishes that the man is a bit of a lech.

    He turns to gape at a girl in tight skimpy shorts. Too
absorbed to look where he's going, he falls into a ditch of
muddy water.

You establish the character, then get a laugh.

3 Take an office setting. A secretary is on the phone having a
very personal conversation with her boyfriend.
    The office creep surreptitiously picks up an extension
phone to listen in.

This tells us his character.

    Then something happens to surprise him so that his
eavesdropping is discovered.
    He may have an uncontrollable sneeze.
    The secretary thinks it's the boyfriend and says: 'Bless you,
darling.'
    The boyfriend, puzzled, says: 'I didn't sneeze.'
    OR:
    When the creep is absorbed in eavesdropping, he doesn't
notice another office worker coming up to him, saying: 'Mr
Perkins, can I use that phone when you've finished?'

Either of these should get a laugh.
    When you have to tell your audience something – think . . .
Is there a visual way of doing it? And, of course, of getting a
laugh.

One good visual is worth pages of dialogue.

9 Characterization

Situation comedy is really character comedy. The comedy should come from the way your characters react to a situation and the way they react to each other.

We see this in *Steptoe and Son*. Harold and his father have their individual attitudes to the outside world, and a love-hate relationship towards each other.

If comedy is based on character, then the stronger the character the stronger the comedy.

Not only do you want strong characters, but your characters should be in sharp contrast to each other. A good example of this is the three friends in *The Golden Girls*. There's Blanche – the man-hungry southern belle; Rose – the small-town middle American, sweet but slow and unworldly; and Dorothy – the responsible one, with a great line in one-liners.

In an ideal script, each character should have a point of view from which to speak.
Lines should not be interchangeable.

A good test for your script is to blot out the names and see if it's obvious from the dialogue which character is saying which line.

There is another test for a character that is worth considering: Do you think that an impressionist could do an impression of that character, as an impressionist might 'do' Alf Garnett.

In developing your format, especially if it's a gang or group show, try and make one of your characters a bit overboard, rather outrageous in contrast to all the other characters, in fact not quite on their wavelength; this can get you extra laughs in most situations.

For an example, let's look again at *The Golden Girls*.

In the first episode, there was a very dramatic scene towards the end of the show:

Blanche's marriage had been called off at the last moment. The girls were sitting round the kitchen table having a midnight snack. Rose and Dorothy were genuine in their sympathy. The scene was played for real, played straight . . . it had to be. Then Dorothy's Mum wandered in to say: 'Careful what you take out of the fridge, I keep my specimens in there.'

This, of course, got a belting laugh and broke the tension, which was just what was needed at that point in the show.

Most group or gang shows can benefit from having one outrageous character. In *Birds of a Feather*, there's Dorien the overdressed, oversexed Jewish neighbour; in *On the Buses* there was Olive.

But in the average sitcom, you don't want too many outrageous charcters, or things would get out of hand and you would lose all reality.

THE DOBERMAN EFFECT
When putting together your show it is also useful to have a cameo part for a really wild over-the-top character. A character like the dumb slob Doberman in *Sergeant Bilko* – a character who can step in, get a few laughs when needed, then get off.

These cameo parts have to be short because the characters are so over-the-top that the humour wouldn't be sustained.

Another Doberman-type character is Klinger in M*A*S*H. He keeps dressing up in women's clothes as he wants to be certified crazy to get his discharge from the Army.

When this rough, tough, usually unshaven, soldier walks in a scene dressed in a low-cut evening gown, it can be very funny, but the gimmick can't be over-used as the joke soon wears thin.

There are many well-drawn cameos in *'Allo 'Allo*, but surely the most original and outrageous one is Crabtree, the British agent disguised as a gendarme, whose atrocious French is conveyed in mangled English.

For example:

> In one episode of *'Allo 'Allo*, someone had to come into the cafe with the important plot line: 'There has been another cock up. The British Air Force has bombed the waterworks.'
> To liven up a plot scene, which was towards the end of the show, the line was given to Crabtree who entered the cafe to say:

CRABTREE: There has been another kick up. The British Air Farce have dropped their bums on the waterwicks.

RENE: (UNBELIEVABLE) On the waterworks?

CRABTREE: Yes. The British farters dropped all their bums on the pimps.

RENE: I think I need a dictionary.

CRABTREE: (GETTING ANNOYED) The pimps! The pimps in the pimping station. No water is being pimped down the poops!

The best use of these cameo characters, or what I call 'Dobermans', is to liven up a quiet scene or a plot scene.

In a way they are the comic relief in a comedy show; very helpful, but not to be over-used.

A writer should strive to create good characters. So many shows are only moderately successful because the characters are uninteresting and the shows come over as bland.

For strong comedy impact there is nothing like strong characters – and, of course, a Doberman.

10   The sitcom – Are there any new ideas?

No, not many. That fantastic new show is very often a different twist or a new angle on a basic theme.

New writers furiously try to dream up an idea that is completely different and original, but mostly the thing that is different and original is the writer's talent.

Take *Fawlty Towers* – The idea of a sitcom set in a badly run hotel is not particularly original. Many versions of it have been done, and that idea has been plonked on the programme controller's desk more often than Valium. But the comic genius, John Cleese, took this hackneyed idea and turned it into a sparkling original, unique success . . . a hit world-wide and a 'cult' in many countries.

Don't despair – Your talent is new – It's all been done before, but not the way you're going to do it:

Take the domestic sitcom. Every season sees another permutation. There's the husband, wife and kids; the middle-aged husband and wife whose kids have left home but keep coming back with problems. There's the wife with no husband and kids; the husband with no wife and kids; single parents with kids; and now, homosexuals with kids.

Every setting seems to have been used for comedy – hospitals in *Surgical Spirit* and *Only When I Laugh*, prisons in *Porridge*, pubs in *Cheers*, a barber's shop in *Desmond's*, and a police-station in *The Thin Blue Line*.

Ideas are ten a penny – Treatment is everything:

Take the idea of three or four retired people living together, or having to tolerate each other for companionship and to avoid loneliness.

In England, this basic idea was developed and became *Last of the Summer Wine* which featured the adventures of four men, retired pensioners of conflicting types who needed each other's company.

In the USA, this same basic idea was developed and became *The Golden Girls* – three mature ladies, widows and divorcees with conflicting personalities living together and managing to stay together in spite of the problems.

Take the idea of two completely contrasting characters living together.

A classic example was *The Odd Couple* – meticulous Felix sharing an apartment with a slob.

An English version of this was *The Liver Birds* – two girls sharing a flat – one well-organized and narrow-minded, the other a scatterbrained raver.

The basic idea cropped up yet again with *Kate and Allie* – two attractive divorcees living together.

The most recent version of this basic idea is *Birds of a Feather*. This series, created by Maurice Gran and Laurence Marks, has two sisters living together – contrasting types and lifestyles. One has money, the other hasn't. The only thing they have in common is that both their husbands are in prison! Having husbands in prison is an inspiration; it somehow gives a modern, contemporary feel to a basic theme.

Also, deprived of their husbands for several years, the girls have sexual problems which give the writers more opportunity for comedy – very modern comedy.

Something else that's new – The times we live in

Today, writers have much more scope. They can write about things which were taboo only a few years ago. The condom joke is practically obligatory; four-letter words seem to be the norm. Comediennes make jokes about periods, and single girls getting pregnant.

Until about 1980, unmarried girls in television comedy could not get pregnant – did not have sex. In fact, girls had no functional parts below the waist! Present-day permissiveness enables writers to give freshness to the same old themes.

Writers are always affected by the times in which they live. This applies to all types of writing. Always has. Think of Shakespeare and Dickens.

So what's new? You are – Your talent:
The idea for a series – the setting, or format as it is called – invariably springs from your individual talent, giving a new contemporary approach to one of the basic themes.

A contemporary approach to basic theme resulted in the amazingly successful award-winning *Drop the Dead Donkey.*

Andy Hamilton:

> We got approached by Alan Yentob who asked us why we hadn't written anything for the BBC recently. He said he would welcome an idea. Well, for a while Guy Jenkin and I nursed the idea of doing an office comedy. We felt that there hadn't been a reasonably convincing office comedy. A comedy that would capture the banal and day-to-day jealousies and problems you would get in an office. Then, having decided to go for an office sitcom, we played around with various ideas of where to set it. Eventually, I'm not quite sure how, we thought if we set it in a newsroom, the characters could quite legitimately talk about the news. We just fancied the idea of doing a sitcom that went out the night after we made it, because we were used to that when we wrote for *Weekending, Roy Huddlines* and *Not the Nine O'Clock News* and we thought that it would give it that extra electricity. The script would be 90 per cent main plot with holes left in for topicalities. We went to the BBC with it, but months went by and we didn't get a tangible response from anybody. So we took it to Seamus Cassidy at Channel Four and they commissioned six scripts within twenty-four hours.

11   *The format*

What is a format?
The format of a sitcom should describe the setting and the background for the series as clearly as possible. And, what's more important, delineate the characters in the greatest possible detail and establish their relationships and attitudes to each other.

How do you develop a format?
Choose a basic idea that appeals to you, then start asking questions.
The format for *On the Buses* was evolved something like this:

1 We decided to write a working-class comedy featuring Reg Varney.
2 What did he do for a living?
3 Shopkeeper? Plumber? Electrician?
    We went through all the possibilities and then decided on a bus driver. We felt the uniform would be useful; immediate recognition would tell the audience quickly much of his character and background. Also, buses were a good, fruitful subject – everybody knows about them; again, little need for explanation.
4 What were his problems?
    Well, there could be an inspector at work who would try to make his life a misery.
5 Was he married or single?
    We thought there could be more fun if he was single, and was always trying to get a girl – without much success.
6 Where did he live? Did he live alone?
    We thought there would be more problems if he lived at home with a rather possessive mother.

7 Who else lived in the house? We needed someone in the house for Reg to clash with; as he was basically a nice cockney guy, he couldn't be in conflict too much with his mum.

We decided to have his sister and brother-in-law living in the house to add some more problems and conflict.

8 Reg needed to have a confidante – a mate.

His conductor was the obvious choice, but his character would have to conflict somewhat with Reg's, so we made him a brash, pushy guy – someone who would often lead Reg astray and cause more problems.

CONFLICT

All the time we were developing the show, the important thing was to ensure that there was enough conflict. The first trick in writing comedy is conflict. Without conflict, a scene is flat. With conflict, however small, it comes to life. It can be acted. Otherwise it's bland and uninteresting.

If there are any rules in comedy, **conflict should be the most essential. Conflict! Conflict! Conflict!**

Where does this conflict come from? It should be built into your format. Your format should have characters who are naturally in conflict with each other: Bosses and workers; husbands and wives; in *Yes Minister*, civil servants and politicians; in *Porridge*, warders and prisoners.

Apart from your format, your story line should put your characters not just in conflict with each other, but with the world outside.

TESTING THE FORMAT:

Having worked out the format, the next worry is, is there sufficient mileage in the idea? Can it be sustained?

The best test of the strength of a format is to see whether you can think up story ideas for the first six episodes. If you can do that, then you can assume that the format has potential.

We did that for *On the Buses*, and when we were confident we took it to Frank Muir, then head of light entertainment at London Weekend Television.

This was the format that was presented:

On the Buses
An idea for a 30-minute situation comedy
by Ronald Wolfe and Ronald Chesney

This series revolves around the day-to-day life of STAN BUTLER. He has been 'on the buses' all his working life. He likes his job, but his good nature is taken advantage of by those at home and at work.
They are:

REGULAR FEATURED CAST:

(AT HOME):

ARTHUR – His brother-in-law, aged about forty. Arthur is petty-minded, routine-conscious and intolerant. He earns less than Stan who contributes much more to the household expenses.

Arthur is a railway booking-clerk at a small local station. The railways have a deficit of millions of pounds a year. By the look on Arthur's face, you'd think it was his money they were losing!

He is a white-collar worker (just about); he considers himself to be superior to Stan.

OLIVE: Arthur's wife/Stan's sister. Always sniffing and coughing; a hypochondriac who spends most of her life in a housecoat and curlers. Constantly bickering with her husband, and finds it hard to manage on Arthur's money. (Good-hearted Stan is always forking out!)

STAN'S MOTHER (a widow) – Stan has supported her since he was a lad. If it wasn't for her, Stan would have married long ago, but he is still a bachelor and his mother schemes to keep him that way! She is a crafty old bird and doesn't want to lose her son or his pay-packet. Not that she would ever admit this. In her cunning way, she takes great care to cause trouble between Stan and any girl he might seem likely to marry.

(THE CHARACTERS STAN MEETS AT WORK):

THE BUS INSPECTOR – Punctilious, precise, tall, poker-faced, officious, efficient, always meticulously consulting his clipboard, stopwatch and schedules.

JACK – the regular conductor on Stan's bus. Jack is not only Stan's regular conductor, but his closest friend. They are usually inseparable, except when Jack has a girl and Stan hasn't (which happens quite often).

Jack is more forceful than Stan. He is very likeable and has an easy way with women. He is a quick thinker – a schemer – and often leads Stan into trouble and makes him the fall-guy. But Stan never complains; he admires Jack and wishes he possessed some of his nerve.

Besides these featured players, there are several characters who have small parts but who appear regularly.

They are:

THE GIRLS IN THE CANTEEN AND WAITRESSES (Usually dated by the busmen)

THE DEPOT MANAGER

OTHER DRIVERS AND CONDUCTORS

OTHER WOMEN DRIVERS AND CONDUCTORS

OFFICE GIRLS AND SECRETARIES

SETS:

There are two basic sets:

The living room/kitchen of the house and a section of the bus depot. These same sets are used each week.

Apart from this format, we presented a detailed story line of a pilot script; this ran to about five or six pages. Also, ideas for the following five episodes.

These were kept brief – just a half-page synopsis to illustrate how the series would develop, and to show the potential.

INSURANCE POLICIES:
Looking back over the format, you can see that it had several 'insurance policies', i.e. built-in sources for comedy:

The domestic situations; the problems at work; problems at

home, and problems when work affected the home life and when home life affected work.

Examples:

Stan has to learn self-defence to deal with hooligans; he has learned the rudiments at work, and this leads to comedy at home when he practises with Arthur.

When Mum and Olive were ill, Stan had to cope with running the house. There were scenes with him stopping the bus to do some shopping and picking stuff up from the launderette (and, of course, getting caught by the Inspector).

Another 'insurance policy' was having a gang-show format with six regular characters. If only three of them had worked, the show would have been moderately well-received. But in this instance, all the six characters were a great success.

The time spent working on the format was well-rewarded. All the 'insurance policies' worked, and there was enough potential for seventy-two episodes and three full-length feature films.

12   *Casting is crucial*

Alan Plater: Casting? . . . It's crucial. If you get it right you
             can forget your worries and get on with the next
             job.

**If you write material that has to be performed, your material
will be judged to a large extent by the person who performs
it.**

Luckily, I had a marvellous example of this early in my
career. I was asked to write a radio script for Dick Emery, a
popular but rather broad comedian. After the broadcast, the
head of light entertainment told me he wasn't exactly
enamoured with the script. In fact, it was rather corny.
    About a year later, I was asked at the very last moment to
provide a script for Eartha Kitt . . . A rush job – no time to
write anything new. So I gave Eartha Kitt practically the same
script I had written for Dick Emery. Eartha did the routine
with great style – a great success. Afterwards, one of the
bosses came over to congratulate me, saying: 'Fantastic, I
didn't know you could write such sophisticated material.

Do writers have any say in choosing the cast?
In my experience, writers are always consulted.

*But what about new writers? Would anybody listen to
them?*
Surprisingly, the answer is YES. Even a new writer has far
more influence than one might think.
    You may be a beginner, but if a producer has bought your
script, which has cost several thousand pounds, is about to
embark on a six-part series that might cost about a million

pounds, or even a one-shot pilot that could cost about a hundred and fifty thousand pounds, of course he is going to listen to your casting suggestions.

How is casting done? What's the process?

As always in this business, there are no rules. But let's look at some case histories and see if we can find some guidelines:

Yes Minister

The BBC were anxious to find a series featuring Paul Eddington, who had done so well for them in *The Good Life*.

Round about that time, Jonathan Lynn teamed up with Antony Jay and they developed an idea for a show about a cabinet minister, which the BBC thought suitable for Eddington.

What about Nigel Hawthorne as Sir Humphrey?

Stuart Allen – producer/director of such shows as *Love Thy Neighbour* and *On the Buses* – was asked to direct the pilot show:

> Many years before, I had directed the television version of the successful stage play *Mrs Wilson's Diary*. Nigel Hawthorne was in that play. I was most impressed by his performance. I always thought he would be marvellous on television if the right part came along. When we were casting *Yes Minister*, I thought he would be absolutely right for Sir Humphrey and, of course, he was.

You might think that Lynn and Jay were lucky to come up with the right idea for the right person at the right time. Yes, they had a certain amount of luck, but all the luck in the world is no good unless you have the talent to back it up. Lynn and Jay certainly had the talent.

Fresh Fields

Yes Minister was written and then cast, but some established writers like John Chapman do their best work when they know exactly who they are writing for:

> I prefer to write for 'names'. I have nearly always known exactly whom I was writing for. I wrote a pilot script with Julia McKenzie in mind. Thames TV liked it, so did Julia, and

it was Julia who suggested she would like to work with Anton Rodgers, so right away we had our two leading parts cast.

This was a classic case of the right writer for the right cast, and *Fresh Fields* was an immediate success and became an award-winning series.

But even established writers can't always get the cast they want. John Chapman and Ray Cooney have had a string of West End theatre successes. Working in collaboration or on their own, they have been responsible for such farces as *Simple Spymen, Dry Rot, Run For Your Wife* and *Move Over Mrs Markham*. They found no actors interested in a play they'd written – *Not Now Darling*:

> Nobody thought it was funny. It did the rounds for over eighteen months. It was read by every actor who might possibly be suitable. They all turned it down. None of them thought it was funny. Then the play was read by Donald Sinden, who loved it and agreed to do it as soon as he was available.
>   Donald was then working in a show with Bernard Cribbins, suggested him for the other leading part. With Sinden and Cribbins in the main roles, the play was a big hit in the West End, had a long run, and has been played in dozens of countries throughout the world ever since.

The odd thing about a stage play is that the initial casting only is crucial. Once the play has been established as a hit, the play will still run successfully in spite of many cast changes. Cast changes are not usually successful on television.

Till Death Us Do Part

There are obvious advantages in writing for well-known comedians, but if the material is controversial there are some problems, as Johnny Speight, creator of the series, found out:

> Alf Garnett was a bigot. So bigoted, he was a figure of fun. He was anti-black, anti-Jew, anti-socialist. No well-known comedian would play such a part. A comedian, to a large extent, plays himself. If he played this part it would alter his accepted personality, it would be bad for his image. We

decided to go for an actor, not a known comedian, because an actor would play the part as written and not worry about his image.

But getting the right actor wasn't easy. Casting is an unpredictable business, especially on television. Schedules have to be met. A show can be scheduled to start even before it is cast. Then there is a question of 'who's available?' There is often a last minute panic, when you can be very unlucky or get very lucky.

Speight was lucky. He ended up with Warren Mitchell:

It was a last minute choice. I know for a fact that Leo McKern was the first choice, but he couldn't be contacted as he was away on a sailing holiday. They were also talking to Peter Sellers and Lionel Jeffries. There were about five people on the list, but nothing was settled. There were just two days to go before the start of rehearsals, so they booked me.

This is where the luck of casting comes in.

Johnny Speight's writing was so strong that the series would have met with some measure of success anyway. But Johnny acknowledges his good fortune in getting Warren Mitchell:

Warren gave it that extra dimension. He fleshed out the part. He gave it so many extra little touches!

Warren Mitchell is a fine dramatic actor. But being a 'class' actor is not in itself enough for comedy. To play comedy you have to have natural flair . . . a natural sense of timing. This is something you are born with.

Often quoted in this business are the last words of that famous actor, Henry Irving. When asked how he felt, the reply was: 'Dying is easy, it's comedy that's difficult.'

Birds of a Feather

This show was created and written by Maurice Gran and Laurence Marks. They have some definite views on casting:

Laurence Marks:

Since about 1985, when we returned from the States, Maurice and I have known who we want to play the leads in our shows before we start writing.

With *Birds of a Feather* the casting came first. We had worked with Pauline Quirke and Linda Robson in *Harvey Moon*, one of our earlier shows. When that show finished we thought that Linda and Pauline were potentially two great stars if only we could find the right vehicle for them.

It wasn't until four years later that we came up with the right situation for them. But we needed one more girl.

Quite by chance I was invited to see a play called *Exclusive Yarns* at the Comedy Theatre, starring Lesley Joseph. Lesley was brilliant. We'd found our Dorien, and that's how *Birds of a Feather* was born.

I think the reason why *Birds of a Feather* worked is that no one remembered the girls Pauline and Linda from *Harvey Moon*.

I always think the key to success in television situation comedy is if the cast is known (i.e. experienced actors), but relatively unknown to the TV audience, because nothing comes to the screen with baggage.

For example, whatever part George Cole plays from now on is really Arthur Daley personified, because you can't get that image out of your mind. All credit to the writer that gave him that persona.

The New Statesman

In this show as well, the casting came first. Laurence Marks relates:

Maurice and I were approached by Rik Mayall, whose previous television character was a spotty youth with a beret in *The Young Ones*.

Rik asked us to create a new character for him. We gave him sophistication and a Savile Row suit, and he became Alan B'Stard.

Men Behaving Badly

Executive producer Beryl Vertue:

I used a casting director, though in actual fact I cast Harry Enfield the first time. For the other male lead Harry Enfield suggested someone called Martin Clunes, and I went to see him in a play at the Regent's Park Open Theatre – a period play – but you could just tell he was very good, so we cast him.

Caroline Quentin and Leslie Ash were chosen from auditions ... the casting director had proposed several people for these roles, when we saw someone we liked we called them back several times and even if they were very famous we got them to read, because it is important to us, and it is important to them.

The director, the writer and I were always at the casting sessions. Some people don't have the writer there at all, but I think that's ridiculous. It is no good presenting the writer with a cast they don't like – someone they don't want to write for – or someone they can't write for.

After the first series we had a cast change. Harry Enfield had only signed for one series. When he left a new flatmate came in, Neil Morrissey.

Butterflies and *Bread*

Carla Lane, creator of both these series, is one writer who hardly ever casts first:

> I don't write with any person in mind. I don't like writing for known people . . . television names . . . unless of course they became names and become known through a series of mine.
>
> I'm not very good at casting . . . I don't think I'm tough enough . . . Interviewing all those actors . . . I'd like to give them all a job.
>
> I leave casting to the director, although I am always called for an opinion on the final choice.

Some writers like to know their cast before writing; some write first and then cast; others cast when they are actually writing.

The Beiderbecke Affair
Alan Plater:

> When I was immersed in the writing and beginning to feel how the part was developing, I rang the producer and said: 'I think we should send this to Jimmy' (James Bolam). The producer agreed and Jimmy liked it. That was it. We had to find a girl to play opposite Jimmy. The producer rang me and

said: 'I have a short list of three, the first one is Barbara Flynn.'

I said, say no more . . . she's the one. I'd worked with her before on *Barchester Chronicles* and I thought she'd be right. She was. The casting was perfect.

When you are writing a two-hander . . . A series with two leads . . . Once one of the leads has been cast, this gives a clue – A strong indication – as to who should play opposite . . . And casting this second lead is relatively easy.

A *Fine Romance* and *Surgical Spirit*

These are just two of the many successful sitcoms produced by Humphrey Barclay, one of Britain's most successful independent producers.

A Fine Romance was written by Bob Larbey and shown to Humphrey Barclay, then head of comedy for London Weekend Television:

> I liked the script, and the casting was simple. Bob Larbey, who wrote the show, suggested Michael Williams for one of the leads. Almost immediately I wondered about Judi Dench. Judi agreed to do it, and they were absolutely right for the show. Unlike casting some shows, there was no agonizing, soul searching, waiting for availability . . . it was simple, it was easy, it worked.
>
> A more recent show of mine, *Surgical Spirit*, presented more problems. The script had been turned down by the BBC. The writer brought it to me, and I liked it and wanted to do it.
>
> But casting the lead . . . a bristly, hot-tempered yet attractive lady surgeon was tricky.
>
> I drew up a short list of about five names which I kept mulling over. I couldn't make up my mind. None of them seemed quite right. Then I was invited to a charity performance – a gala concert – and saw Nichola McAuliffe singing 'I Hate Men', and I knew right away that she was the lady I was looking for.

Funny on stage – but what about TV?

Less experienced people can sometimes be fooled when they see an actor in a stage play getting laugh after laugh, and assume they have great potential on television.

Be wary, check out the actor; he might have been on tour with the play for several weeks and, no doubt helped by the director, has learnt where the laughs come and how to get laughs in that particular play.

A television series is quite different. It requires a different talent. The actor is presented with a new script each week . . . he has no time to play around with it, or experiment.

To survive the treadmill of a long-running TV series, the actor has to have this inborn sense of comedy. He has to 'know' where the laughs are, and how to time them. If not, your script is not going to work as well as it might, and I'm afraid that the writer will get much of the blame.

Should a new writer make cast suggestions when
submitting a script?
Yes, it might help, and there's a reason why, according to Johnny Speight:

> I know writers starting out will find this very hard to believe, but there are very few people in the business who are good readers of scripts.
>
> This goes for so many TV executives, producers and directors. They read a script and only see a laugh if the line is an obvious joke line. Few of them can visualize a script, imagine how it will play, and where the laughs come . . . but it does help them if you say this is a Penelope Keith part or a David Jason part; they imagine these known strong personalities saying the lines and it helps visualize the script.

But don't write a script that is so tailormade that it can only be played by one star – a famous bankable star.
You may have written a script that is absolutely right for David Jason. The TV company may want to do it, David Jason may love and want to do it, but the handful of bankable stars are in great demand and may be under all sorts of contracts and not available for years.

If you want to make cast suggestions, it is much safer to write your script so that the lead parts can be played by any one of five or six actors of the same type; you can suggest them. This gives casting more flexibility, and helps those trying to visualize your script.

From these examples, it is clear that there is not just one way of casting a show. Sometimes it is a mixed combination of all the possibilities we discussed.

This is what happened with *On the Buses*.

There were six parts to be cast:

STAN – **the lead part**
We went in with the following list:

1 Ronnie Barker
2 Reg Varney
3 Bernard Cribbins

Reg Varney was our number one choice, so we put him second. We'd found from experience that TV executives treat a list of names a bit like choosing from the wine list; they're a bit suspicious of the first, and usually plump for the second. Somehow they feel it is 'safer' and not too expensive. (Note: There is much more to writing than putting words on paper!)

As for the parts of the inspector and the conductor Jack, our director Stuart Allen cast Stephen Lewis and Bob Grant who had worked with him in *Mrs Wilson's Diary*.

Doris Hare was everyone's favourite to play Mum – there was no arguing, no agonizing . . . the only problem was, she wasn't available for months. Cicely Courtnedge was booked to play Mum for the first series, then Doris took over; strangely enough, very few viewers seemed to notice.

Michael Robbins was chosen to play the part of Arthur through the usual sort of accident. Some of us were watching another show and spotted Michael doing a small part in *The Harry Worth Show* . . . it was only a cameo part, but he did it magnificently.

The hardest part to cast was Olive. It really is very difficult to find young actresses to play unattractive parts. Then we thought of Anna Karen, a very attractive girl who was actually a most attractive long-legged dancer trying to make it as an actress. In fact, at that time she was doing a one-line part in another show we were doing at the Beeb. With the help of a wig, glasses and padding, she was playing a worn-out, washed-out waitress.

An appointment was fixed for her to meet our director. We

waited at reception for her. Anna, being a woman, glided in dressed to kill – beautifully made-up, with false eyelashes, eyeliner, mascara – the lot!

We knew she'd never get the part looking like that, so we dragged her out to the car, pushed her in the back, and told her to get rid of all the make-up.

Now when Anna is asked how she got the part, she says: 'The writers pushed me into the back of the car and told me to take everything off.'

Baldrick in Blackadder
How Tony Robinson was cast:

I was actually discovered for the British sitcom on three different occasions.

I was originally discovered by Humphrey Barclay when he was making the first *Doctor* series. I got down to the last three, then they cast Barry Evans.

But I did the odd episode . . . one actually written by Jonathan Lynn and George Layton. But after that, nothing much happened.

Playing at Chichester, I was then discovered again by Denis Main Wilson (director of *Till Death*). I did two BBC pilots, but again nothing much happened.

What I didn't know was that John Howard Davies had seen me in a bit part in a series made at Bristol, and John wrote me down in his list of people doing small parts who were vaguely humorous.

Then Richard Curtis and Rowan Atkinson wrote this pilot for Rowan's new series *Blackadder*.

There was a small part in it . . . about six lines only. It was turned down by many. John Howard Davies suggested me, and I took it because I had this burning ambition to take part in this Oxbridge type of comedy, though I would have taken it anyway as I had been out of work for months.

Baldrick just grew. Given the elaborate style in which Rowan was going to talk, it was actually very useful to have somebody very laconic.

In the first series, Baldrick was very crafty, though his schemes tended not to work.

After the first series, Ben Elton joined the writing team and it was Ben's idea to make him absolutely brainless. From then on, the character really took off.'

Writers as well as producers and directors should always be on the lookout for talent.

Alan Plater:

> I have a permanent imaginary notebook. Whenever I go to the theatre or watch something on the box, I'm filing away thinking: 'Yes, he seems interesting . . . she seems interesting . . .' though it may be some time before I want them. Casting is a mixture of memory and instinct.

For comedy writers, casting is part of the job.

Casting for *Drop the Dead Donkey* was a long, painstaking, arduous task.

Andy Hamilton:

> Guy Jenkin and I were totally involved in the casting, because we were also the producers on *Dead Donkey*. The casting process really was exhausting. For eight parts we saw about a hundred and fifty people. Then we whittled them down to the three best for each part. Then we dragged these poor sods in for reading after reading which is nerve-racking for an actor. But, we were determined to give ourselves the best possible choice. We kept calling them back because we needed to know more about them. It was very painful and a terrible ordeal for the actors, but it was terribly useful, because we wanted to see how resilient they were as people. It was all worthwhile because we have never had any problems with the actors. With a big cast we knew it would be a disaster if someone didn't fit in. They were all very much 'let's get on with it and have a good time' actors. We have never had any problems with performer 'angst' on the show.

13 *Writing an episode step by step*

One of the most successful episodes ever of *On the Buses* was entitled 'New Uniforms', it has been repeated again and again.

Let me take you through the process, showing how the script was developed from the starting-point which was just one word.

When we were writing *On the Buses*, we had a list of possible subjects in our notebook. Somewhere on the list was the word 'uniforms'. After writing about thirty episodes, we decided the time had come to do something about uniforms. Our thinking went something like this:

UNIFORMS? What's the angle?
What are the possibilities?
Are the busmen not wearing their regulation uniforms? Maybe they prefer bomber jackets and trainers.
Are they wearing their uniforms to do some dirty DIY jobs at home?
What about new uniforms? The company wants to smarten up its image, so they've ordered some new uniforms . . . designer uniforms.
Yes – NEW UNIFORMS . . . They would look visually good; that was it. The decision was made.

The next step was to hammer out the story line and, as always, it was a question of asking questions.

Would all the busmen be wearing new uniforms?
No – in the first instance, just our star Reg Varney, as Stan Butler, and Jack his conductor.

Now where do we start the show?

> We could start with them actually wearing the new uniforms
> – but no . . . that would be too early; there must be a scene or
> two before that.

We decided that in the opening scene Stan and Jack would
be picked to try out the new uniforms as guinea-pigs because
they were the scruffiest, most slovenly bus crew.

(Note: In fact, Stan Butler, played by Reg Varney, was far
from scruffy; he was always neatly dressed – but not this
week. In a long-running series you have to have a bit of poetic
licence.)

This is how the actual script started:

> FADE UP AFTER OPENING CAPTIONS. VTR SHOT OF BUS COMING
> INTO DEPOT.
>
> SCENE ONE (STUDIO) INT. DEPOT (DAY)
>
> THE NUMBER ELEVEN BUS HAS JUST ARRIVED AFTER ITS RUN.
> THE INSPECTOR IS WAITING FOR STAN AND JACK AS THEY GET
> OFF.
>
> STAN AND JACK LOOK THEIR SCRUFFIEST; THEIR UNIFORMS ARE
> STAINED AND TORN, AND POCKETS BULGING.
>
> THE INSPECTOR IS STANDING, NOTING DOWN THE NUMBER OF
> THE BUS AND WRITING IT DOWN ON HIS CLIPBOARD.

INSP:	Just a minute you two . . . I want you . . . THEY GO TO THE INSPECTOR.
INSP:	I want to speak to you about your uniforms. You scruffy, dirty pair of layabouts. (POINTS TO STAN) What have you been doing? Sleeping in it?
JACK:	Only when he's driving.
INSP:	(POINTS TO ONE OF STAN'S JACKET POCKETS, WHICH IS BULGING AND OUT OF WHICH WE CAN SEE A DIRTY, FILTHY RAG HANGING) What's that stuffed in your pocket?

STAN: (PULLING OUT A BUNCH OF FILTHY RAGS) Just a few rags ... I need those to clean the windscreen.

INSP: The company supply proper cleaning cloths. How dare you stuff such revolting things in their uniform? They can be thrown away for a start ... (HE TAKES THE RAGS FROM STAN)

STAN: (PULLING BACK ONE OF THE RAGS – A BIT CLEANER THAN THE REST) Hang on ... that's my handkerchief ...

INSP: The company will not have disgusting, revolting objects put in its uniforms.

STAN: Don't know why ... they put you in one!
               STAN AND JACK LAUGH.

There followed a short routine about things found in Stan's pockets.

Then the scene ended like this:

STAN: What's all the fuss about our uniforms?

INSP: The company has decided to try out a new type of uniform, and they've decided that you two should be the guinea-pigs.

JACK: I resent the implication ...

STAN: Why pick on us?

INSP: Because you're the scruffiest, untidiest busmen in the depot. If the new uniforms last two weeks on you, they should last two years on anyone else!
               THE INSPECTOR DETACHES TWO PRINTED FORMS FROM HIS CLIPBOARD.

INSP: Here ... they've got to be specially made ... so you've got to fill in your measurements on these forms ... and I want 'em back tomorrow morning.

Note: The measurements for the uniforms could of course have been done at the bus depot. But *On the Buses* was a gang show, based partly on domestic troubles at home and partly on problems at work.

The difficulty with a gang show is to work all the regular cast into the story each week.

If we did not go back home for the measuring routine,

there would be no domestic scene that week and, conse-
quently, nothing for Olive, Arthur and Mum. And further-
more, we thought it would be funnier to have Stan measured
up by the short-sighted, not very bright Olive. Here is an
abridged version of the next scene:

SCENE TWO (KITCHEN) INT. (DAY)

THE NEXT MORNING – BREAKFAST TIME.

MUM AND OLIVE ARE IN THEIR DRESSING-GOWNS. ARTHUR IS AT
THE TABLE, EATING HIS CEREAL. OLIVE IS RUMMAGING AROUND
IN A CHEST OF DRAWERS. STAN IS DRESSED BUT WITHOUT HIS
JACKET. HE IS WAITING TO BE MEASURED.

OLIVE:	I can't find my tape measure anywhere.
ARTHUR:	You were using it in bed last night.
STAN:	(REACTS, SURPRISED) Using it in bed?!
OLIVE:	I was using it to measure my knitting.
STAN:	Knitting in bed?
OLIVE:	I always knit myself to sleep, don't I, Arthur?
ARTHUR:	Always!
MUM:	Don't you keep Arthur awake, love?
OLIVE:	Oh no . . . he was doing his pools.
STAN:	You knitting . . . him doing pools . . . Right orgy you were having . . .
OLIVE:	Here's the tape measure . . . it was in my pocket all the time.
STAN:	Here, Olive . . . measure my arms . . . from the middle of my back . . . Mum, you write it down.
	OLIVE MEASURES STAN'S ARM FROM THE BACK; HE HOLDS IT UP.
OLIVE:	Right arm . . . 28 inches.
	SHE SHOWS STAN WHERE SHE IS HOLDING TAPE. SHE MEASURES THE LEFT ARM.
OLIVE:	Left arm . . . 32 inches.
STAN:	What are you talking about? I haven't got one arm longer than the other . . .
ARTHUR:	It wouldn't surprise me.
OLIVE:	SHOWING TAPE WITH HER FINGER ON THE MARK There's my finger . . . look . . .
STAN:	How can I have one arm longer than the other?
MUM:	Perhaps it's driving the bus . . . you know, driving with one hand on the gear lever . . .

STAN: Don't be daft, mum.

MUM: I remember when you were little, you did have one ear sticking out more than the other . . .

STAN: Not four inches.

OLIVE: (HOLDS UP TAPE MEASURE) I still make it the same . . .

                STAN LOOKS AGAIN AT THE TAPE THAT OLIVE IS HOLDING, STILL WITH HER FINGER ON THE MARK.

STAN: Show me that . . . (SUDDENLY REALIZING) You've measured it from the wrong end! From seventy-two inches downwards.

Note: The measuring routine went on for another couple of minutes, and then we had to stop because there are only so many laughs you can get about Olive and the tape measure without going over the top.

But we still needed the domestic spot to be longer to balance the show and, as always, we found the answer from thinking about our characters and their attitudes.

The scene continued . . .

                THE MEASURING WAS DONE AND MUM WAS SERVING BREAKFAST.

ARTHUR: I'm getting a bit fed up with the way I'm being treated in this family.

                MUM COMES TO THE TABLE WITH TWO PLATES, ON WHICH ARE TWO SAUSAGES EACH AND BACON.

MUM: Now, now . . . you know I always treat you like one of my own . . .

ARTHUR: Yes . . . then why are my sausages smaller than his?

                ARTHUR POINTS TO STAN'S PLATE.

MUM: Oh, are they? I'm sorry, dear . . . I thought I'd given you equal shares . . .

ARTHUR: You have . . . he's got more sausage, and I've got more grease!

STAN: Oh, don't take any notice, mum . . . he's being childish . . . those sausages are the same size.

ARTHUR: I'm not being childish. It was the same yesterday with the brussel sprouts.

STAN: Oh, we're not having that again . . .

ARTHUR: The fact remains, you had thirteen, and I only had nine!

STAN:	Oh Blimey, we'd better settle this before he starts counting the baked beans. Here, Olive, give us that tape measure . . .
MUM:	What you going to do?
STAN:	Measure his sausage!
	STAN MEASURES ARTHUR'S SAUSAGE, AND THEN HIS OWN, VERY QUICKLY.
ARTHUR:	(GRIMLY) There you are . . . yours is four-and-a-half inches; mine's nearly an inch less.
STAN:	That's because yours is bent.
	STAN STRAIGHTENS OUT THE SAUSAGE ON ARTHUR'S PLATE WITH HIS FINGERS.
ARTHUR:	Take your finger out of my food! What do you think you're doing?
STAN:	Straightening out your sausages . . . (STAN MEASURES SAUSAGE) There, it's exactly the same! Now admit you were wrong!
ARTHUR:	It may be as long, but it's much thinner . . .
STAN:	Gawd! You obstinate cuss . . .
MUM:	It looks thinner because it's darker; Olive looks much thinner when she's dressed in dark colours.
ARTHUR:	I've never noticed!
STAN:	It's just the same . . . All right, you don't trust me . . . (HE PICKS UP THE SAUSAGE) Here Olive, measure this round the top.
ARTHUR:	(NOW VERY CROSS) Will you put my sausage down!
OLIVE:	I don't want to get the measure dirty.
ARTHUR:	The measure! What about my breakfast?
STAN:	Give it here . . .
	STAN GOES TO MEASURE ROUND THE SAUSAGE.
ARTHUR:	(GETS UP) Right . . . I've had enough . . . You can chuck that away . . . it's contaminated.
MUM:	Oh, no, Arthur.
ARTHUR:	I'm not having that measure round my sausage after it's been round his trousers. (PUSHING PLATE AWAY) I'm not eating this . . .
MUM:	That wasn't very hygienic, Stan . . . (TO ARTHUR) Tell you what, Arthur, I've got a couple of fish fingers left over . . . I'll warm them up for you.
STAN:	(HANDING MEASURE TO MUM) Better measure them fish fingers, mum – otherwise he'll say you've given him one finger and one thumb!

The scene continued with more groans from the petty-minded Arthur.

It is interesting to note that if your characters are strong enough they will take over a scene and help you write it.

This domestic scene turned out to be quite strong, so we only needed one more short scene before the commercial break. This was:

SCENE THREE (DEPOT) INT. (DAY)

IN THIS SCENE THE INSPECTOR, STAN AND JACK ARRIVE WITH THEIR MEASUREMENTS AND THE INSPECTOR SHOWS THEM THE DESIGN OF THE NEW UNIFORM FOR THE FIRST TIME. A LARGE SKETCH IS PINNED TO THE WALL.

STAN AND JACK ARE HORRIFIED. THE NEW UNIFORMS ARE WAY OVER THE TOP – RIDICULOUS – THEY REFUSE TO WEAR THEM.

THE INSPECTOR SAYS, 'THAT'S WHAT THE MANAGEMENT WANTS, AND IF YOU DON'T WEAR THEM YOU'RE FIRED!'

Note: Part One ended with a threat of trouble.

COMMERCIAL BREAK

PART TWO

SCENE FOUR INT. (DAY).

FADE UP ON THE CANTEEN.

AT LEAST A DOZEN BUSMEN ARE GATHERED SITTING AROUND. STAN AND JACK COME OUT OF THE MEN'S ROOM. THEY ARE DRESSED IN THE NEW UNIFORMS. THE UNIFORMS ARE OVER THE TOP. TOO SMART, TOO MUCH BRAID, ETC. ETC.
THEY ARE SELF-CONSCIOUS, EMBARRASSED.
THEY ARE GREETED BY WOLF WHISTLES AND CAT CALLS, HOOTING, ETC.

THE SCENE CONTINUED FOR THREE OR FOUR MINUTES. THERE WAS A BARRAGE OF INSULTS FROM THE OTHER BUSMEN, THEN FROM JACK AND STAN.

AFTER DEALING WITH THE INSULTS, STAN AND JACK PUT SOME

CANTEEN TABLES TOGETHER LIKE A CATWALK AND STRUT UP AND DOWN, SHOWING OFF THEIR NEW UNIFORMS AS MALE MODELS MIGHT DO AT A FASHION SHOW.

THIS ROUTINE IS INTERRUPTED BY THE INSPECTOR COMING IN. HE IS MOST CONCERNED THAT THE NEW UNIFORMS ARE NOT SOILED IN ANY WAY ON THEIR FIRST DAY BEFORE THE MANAGE-MENT SEE THEM.

STAN AND JACK SIT DOWN AT A TABLE.

THE CANTEEN GIRL PUTS A COUPLE OF PLATES, LOADED WITH CANTEEN LUNCH, DOWN ON A TABLE NEAR STAN AND JACK.

GIRL: There's your lunches, Stan.

STAN: Thanks. Come on, Jack . . . I'm famished.

INSP: (GOING BERSERK) You're not going to eat in those clothes?

STAN: What are you talking about? Come on, Jack . . .
STAN IS ABOUT TO SIT DOWN. THE INSPECTOR HOLDS HIM BACK.

INSP: Be careful! (ALMOST TEARFUL) Oh, you would choose that . . . Spaghetti Bolognaise.

STAN: (TAKES A MOUTHFUL AND GETS SOME ON HIS CHIN) Oh, stop fussing.
STAN TAKES ANOTHER MOUTHFUL. HE HAS A LONG PIECE OF SPAGHETTI WITH GRAVY ON IT, AND STARTS SUCKING IT UP.

INSP: No . . . No . . . it's dripping. (HE HOLDS HIS HAND UNDER THE SPAGHETTI UNTIL IT IS SAFELY IN STAN'S MOUTH) You did that on purpose, didn't you? Here – wipe your chin . . .
THE INSPECTOR DABS STAN'S CHIN.

INSP: If you drop any of that brown sauce on that light-grey jacket, it'll show . . .

STAN: Hang on . . . I'll see if they've got some light-grey sauce . . .!!!

INSP: I'm responsible for these uniforms until they've been approved. Here . . . tuck this round your chin.
THE INSPECTOR TAKES A TEACLOTH FROM A TRAY ON THE ADJACENT TABLE AND TUCKS IT UNDER STAN'S CHIN.

INSP: That sauce is dripping off your chin.

This led into a routine with the inspector fussing round Stan while he was eating, rather like an anxious mother fussing round a messy, naughty child.

Scene four ended with Stan and Jack unable to enjoy their meal and walking out, going to a nearby cafe to eat in peace.

We were about three-quarters of the way through the show and we now needed about another five or six minutes of script.

But we felt that all the jokes and permutations about new uniforms had been done.

We needed a twist – a new angle.

From experience we knew that at this stage of the script it's helpful to get your regular characters into a new setting, or to introduce some new characters.

We actually did both.

For Scene Five we moved into a new set and introduced new characters:

SCENE FIVE (CAFE) INT. (DAY).

(ABOUT HALF AN HOUR LATER.)

MIX TO INTERIOR OF SMALL CAFE. JUST A FEW TABLES. STAN AND JACK – IN NEW UNIFORMS – HAVE FINISHED THEIR SNACK. THE EMPTY PLATES ARE ON THE TABLE. THEY'RE MUSING OVER A CUP OF TEA.

STAN:	Let's face it mate; we look a couple of berks tarted up like this . . .
JACK:	Don't worry . . . I'll take it up with the union . . . We're supposed to look like busmen – not Peruvian postmen!
STAN:	(SUDDENLY DRAWING JACK'S ATTENTION) Those two birds are eyeing us. STAN POINTS TO TWO SEXY-LOOKING GIRLS SITTING AT ANOTHER TABLE. THEY ARE LOOKING AT THE BOYS, WHISPERING AND GIGGLING.
JACK:	Fat chance we stand in this stupid clobber. ONE OF THE GIRLS GETS UP AND COMES TOWARDS THEM. THE TWO GIRLS ARE SWEDISH AU PAIRS.
INGRID:	(WITH FOREIGN ACCENT) Hey . . . we are having

	trouble with the money . . . how much is worth this coin in your English money?
	SHE SHOWS THEM A FOREIGN COIN.
STAN:	Sorry love . . . no idea.
INGRID:	Oh, we thought you would know as you are airline pilots.
STAN:	Airline pilots?!
INGRID:	Yes . . . we thought because of your uniform.
STAN:	Oh, no . . . we're not pilots, we're . . .
JACK:	(CUTTING HIM SHORT) No, no . . . you're quite right, darling; what he meant was, we're not both pilots . . . he's a pilot . . . I'm a navigator. That's right, isn't it, Stan?

CUT TO STAN.
C.U. OF SLOW SMILE AS HE CATCHES ON.

STAN:	(CATCHING ON) Oh, yes . . .
JACK:	What money is that?
INGRID:	Swedish. Do you know it? (EAGERLY) Do you fly to Sweden?
JACK:	No . . . er . . . we're on the New York run . . .
STAN:	(STARTLED) Are we?
INGRID:	Oh, New York. Oh, I must tell Birgit . . .
JACK:	Ask her to come and join us . . .
INGRID:	Oh, yes . . .
	INGRID GOES OFF TO BIRGIT.
STAN:	But I don't know anything about flying . . .
JACK:	You went on that holiday charter to Majorca – you saw what went on . . .
STAN:	I didn't. I was sloshed going out – and sick coming back . . .
JACK:	Leave it to me.
	INGRID COMES BACK WITH BIRGIT.
INGRID:	This is Birgit . . . I am Ingrid.
JACK:	This is Stan Butler . . . er . . . Captain Butler. (SHOT OF STAN SMIRKING) I'm Jack Harper.
STAN:	He's a captain, too! Will you sit down?
INGRID:	Oh, it must be marvellous to fly a plane . . . is it very difficult?
STAN:	Nothing to it . . . just like driving a bus.
	THEY ALL LAUGH.
INGRID:	(TO JACK) Did you come from New York today? In this bad weather?

JACK:	Yes . . . we had a very bumpy trip, didn't we, Stan? (STAN IS NOT LISTENING – HE IS LOOKING AT BIRGIT) I said we had a bumpy trip this morning.
STAN:	Yeah, well . . . the high street was up. Er . . . well . . .
INGRID:	High street?
JACK:	Er . . . that's what we call the air lane from London to New York . . . we do it so often . . .
BIRGIT:	I think your work must be very dangerous . . .
JACK:	It is with him at the controls! THE GIRLS LAUGH.

The scene continued with fun from the boys' deception of being airline pilots and it ended with them making a date to take the girls out that night.

We made the girls Swedish au pairs because English girls would not have been fooled. They would know immediately by accents, manners, that Stan and Jack were not pilots. With Swedish girls it was more acceptable.

So we come to the last scene in the show.

SCENE SIX (DEPOT) INT. (DAY).

MIX TO NEXT MORNING IN THE DEPOT.

JACK IN HIS NEW UNIFORM IS WAITING BY THE PLATFORM FOR STAN TO ARRIVE.

STAN ARRIVES, VERY JAUNTY.

| STAN: | Morning, Jack — these uniforms work a treat with the birds. How did you get on last night? |
| JACK: | (YAWNING CONTENTEDLY) Marvellous. |

Stan and Jack discuss what happened last night with the girls. There is some fun and conflict from their characters because Jack always does much better with the girls than Stan, who is a little timid and shy with the opposite sex. However, they mostly agree that the new uniforms are marvellous and they want to keep them. They will, of course, wear them for another date that night with the Swedish girls.

The inspector comes bustling up:

INSP: Here, you two . . . stop lolling about there . . . you've got to get out of them new uniforms.

STAN: What?

INSP: You two put the poison in so much that none of the other busmen will wear them. The management are dropping the whole idea. Like you said . . . they do look ridiculous . . . So go and change back into your old uniforms.

THEY PROTEST, BUT THE INSPECTOR INSISTS.

MIX TO FIVE MINUTES LATER.
THE INSPECTOR IS PACING UP AND DOWN BY THE SIDE OF THE BUS, WAITING FOR STAN AND JACK.

A BUSMAN GOES BY.

INSP: Hey . . . tell those two layabouts, Butler and his mate, to get a move on . . . their bus is late out.

THE BUSMAN GOES OFF. AS HE DOES, INGRID AND BIRGIT APPEAR ROUND THE FRONT OF THE BUS.

This is perfectly acceptable. The depot is not just a garage but a point for passengers to board.

THE GIRLS APPROACH THE INSPECTOR.

INGRID: (IN ACCENT) You are the Inspector . . . yes?

INSP: Yes, madam . . . can I help you?

INGRID: We wish to go to the museum. What bus is for there?

INSP: You'll have to catch the number nine . . . it'll be coming in . . . (HE LOOKS UP HIS CLIPBOARD) . . . three minutes. You get off at Ackers Street . . . and then turn left for the museum.

STAN AND JACK APPEAR ROUND THE END OF THE BUS, LOOKING MORE SCRUFFY THAN EVER IN THEIR CRUMPLED OLD UNIFORMS

STAN: All right, Blakey, here we are . . . (SUDDENLY SPOTS THE GIRLS) Cor Blimey! (TO JACK) Look . . . what do we do now?

CUT TO THE GIRLS AND THE INSPECTOR
THEY HAVE SPOTTED THE LADS

INGRID: Birgit! Look . . . our friends. Why are they dressed like that?

INSP: Your friends? Those two?

INGRID: I do not understand . . . they said they were airline pilots.

JACK: Well, it was all a bit of a mix-up.

STAN: Yes, that's right . . . what with them being Swedish and all that . . .

BIRGIT: Are you not Captain Butler?

INGRID: And you are not Captain Harper?

INSP: (MORE AND MORE INTRIGUED – ENJOYING THEIR DISCOMFORT) Captain Butler? Captain Harper? What have you been telling these girls?

INGRID: Do they not fly the jumbo jet plane to New York? (SHE PRONOUNCED IT 'CHUMBO CHET' – WHICH WAS QUITE AMUSING)

INSP: (MIMICKING) Chumbo Chet? They can't even get the bus to the cemetery gates.
THE GIRLS STALK OFF.

INSP: (CHORTLING) Captain Butler? That stretches the imagination. Well, you're cleared for take-off . . . so if you'd like to climb into your cockpit, you can taxi out into the high street and set course for the cemetery. Come on, both of you . . . hop on to the Jumbo! Coo! This has made my day.
HE GOES OFF.

ROLL END CAPTIONS AS STAN GOES ROUND TO FRONT OF BUS, AND JACK GETS ON PLATFORM.

THE END

This script worked quite well, and is often shown as a Comedy Classic.

RECAP
The story line was developed from the idea of NEW UNIFORMS.

We started with the idea of new uniforms, then, working backwards, added on the measuring scene, and, before that, arrival at the depot looking scruffy.

To end the story, we went out to the cafe and met the girls. This gave us another couple of scenes, making six scenes altogether.

While there are no rules, most of the scripts we wrote for this series had six scenes, three before the break and three after.

14   *What are we going to write about this week?*

In a sitcom series which runs for several seasons, you are going to need at least 13, or 26, or maybe 39 (or even more) story lines.

But where do all these ideas come from?

Here are some of the ways you can approach this problem:

ASSOCIATION
Make a list of subjects associated with your format.

When we started to write *On the Buses*, we made a list of possible plot ideas such as:

> Strikes
> Canteens
> New uniforms
> Radio control
> First aid
> Lost property

There were at least twenty ideas – and most of them were successfully developed into story lines, very much described in 'Hammering out the story line' (p. 46).

I am sure that when Jimmy Perry and David Croft started to write *Dad's Army*, they made a list with such items as:

> Manoeuvres
> Bomb disposal
> Guarding prisoners
> Rationing

Most shows with a strong format will have plot possibilities which are peculiar to that show, and that show only.

But there are also many standard subjects that can be applied to most formats, and although the subject is the same the final script is quite different because the format, cast and, of course, the writers are different.

Here is an example:

Trying to stop smoking
This topic has been used again and again in so many sitcoms; you know the sort of thing.

The husband or the boss getting bad-tempered and irritable as he fights the craving.

It is a very standard plot, yet the same topic used by the writers of *Yes Prime Minister* resulted in a brilliant satirical episode, taking the angle that if the Government banned smoking it would lose revenue, with the Prime Minister torn between banning smoking on health grounds and losing millions of pounds from the duty on tobacco.

Whatever the format, it is always well worth considering some of the standard subjects. Here are some of the good old standbys:

Holidays
Illness
Dieting
Anniversaries
Christmas
Weddings
Shortage of money
Babies

You can easily add to this list by looking through the popular press and magazines.

Note the subject matter of the features and articles. You will find the same topics again and again.

Now *Holidays* may seem too broad a canvas for a half-hour sitcom; the subject has so many aspects. That is absolutely true, so this is what you do:

Pick just one aspect of the subject which has possibilities for your show.

For example:

If your star is a worrier, a neurotic type, say, like Richard Briers, there's a lot of mileage to be got by the locking up of the house, then unlocking it and locking it again and again to check that the water and gas and other appliances are turned off.
OR:
Losing the tickets and passports, which leads to complications.
OR:
If your show features a young married couple, perhaps we have them arrive at a small Spanish hotel, to find all the rooms are double-booked and they have to share with other couples – which leads to complications of a different kind.

Another good starting-point for story lines is to make a list of your characters and, beside each name, write:

What does he/she want?
What are his/her problems?

Wherever you can, it is always best to slant your story to a personal relationship.

In a show like *Dynasty*, there are always some high-powered business transactions. But how many people really understand all these intrigues between stockholders? I am sure that the vast audience is more interested in what goes on in the bedroom than what goes on in the boardroom.

People are interested in people – their desires, failings, weaknesses, especially, it seems, their weaknesses.
Many highly successful and powerful men often remain almost completely unknown to the general public until they get involved in a juicy divorce, or have a fling with a girl who decides to 'kiss and sell'. A newspaper editor gets out his cheque book, and there's a headline in the tabloid: 'CONFESSIONS OF A TYCOON'S TART'. Circulation goes up,

and this is probably the only thing about the tycoon that the general public will ever remember.

A plot based on a personal emotion is always worth considering.

One week, in an episode of *Dad's Army*, we found Arthur Lowe as Captain Mainwaring, a middle-aged man, infatuated with a charming lady. The affair, of course, came to nothing. The story was very funny – very sad – and quite touching, and proved to be one of the best and well-remembered episodes of the series, but yet it had very little to do with the basic format of the show which was about a Home Guard unit in World War Two as they waited on the coast for the German invasion.

WRITE WHAT YOU KNOW ABOUT

If your format is based or derived from personal experience (which is always good) you are likely to have a plentiful supply of story lines.

The first TV sitcom that Chesney and I wrote was set in a dressmaking factory. The one reason for the success of the show – *The Rag Trade* – was that we really knew what we were writing about. The setting was authentic and realistic. It made a refreshing change to the normal cosy middle-class sitcom. Chesney at one time had a business share in a clothing factory, while I had worked on the bench in a factory making radio equipment.

From my experiences there, I always thought there would be a good series about factory life.

We had to clock-in every morning – the workers hated that time clock. We used to lose money if we were late. There were various ways of cheating the time clock: sometimes we would squirt glue into the clock to slow it down; other times we would arrange for a couple of the lads to get in early and clock in the rest of us who staggered in later.

There was cheating again at going-home time; some of us would sneak off early through the back fence, whilst our friends would clock us out at the right going-home time.

Fiddling the clock was great fun, especially on the night shift. We'd clock-in at eight o'clock at night, sneak out, go home and come back at six a.m., creep in and pretend we'd been working all night.

When work got a bit boring we'd disappear into the toilets for a smoke and chat, or sit in the cubicles for a quiet read, do our football pools or have a little snooze. The management – worried about low production – tried to time the workers in and out of the toilets. The workers immediately called a lightning strike, and there was even less production.

But life in the factory didn't just consist of skiving; there was also pilfering, petty larceny, and romantic assignations between the factory boys and girls, which usually took place in the field behind the factory, during working hours of course.

With our personal recollections, we were never short of story lines for *The Rag Trade*. It started on the BBC with thirty-nine episodes, was revived later by London Weekend Television for twenty-two episodes, and is now successfully running in Scandinavia.

The secret of that show was that not only were we writing what we knew about, but that many of our viewers worked in factories and could identify with the situations.

There was a similar approach in another show of ours – *Meet the Wife*.

The show was based on day by day happenings of a married couple – Thora Hird and Freddie Frinton, a plumber. Practically everything that happened to them in the series has happened to most married couples.

The pilot script 'The Bed', on which the show sold, was simple and a little sentimental. It was their twenty-fifth wedding anniversary and, now that they had a bit of money, Thora wanted a new bed.

In fact, the show opened with Thora and Fred in bed . . . the bed they'd had for twenty-five years; old, creaky, with a sagging mattress.

But on the first night in their new bed they had a row. Fred went off to sleep on his own in the spare room – in the old bed – taking most of the blankets with him. Thora, rummaging around for some blankets, found the anniversary present that Fred had hidden, and a love letter – probably the only one he'd ever written to her. Brushing away a tear, Thora tiptoed to the spare room and quietly crept into the old bed to snuggle up to Fred – in that creaky old bed, just as we'd found them at the start of the show.

Yes, the story is rather simple, but it must have touched a nerve because that episode was rated by the BBC as one of the most popular shows in the Comedy Playhouse series.

The other most popular episode in that series was called 'The Ring'. This story really worked because it was based on something that we've all done – losing something, then looking through the dustbin to see if it's been thrown away.

Fred came home to find Thora distraught. She'd taken off her ring when she was cleaning the oven, and now she could not find it. They searched all round the house. No luck.

In the middle of the night, Thora had an idea. The ring might have dropped to the floor, got swept up and put in the dustbin. They decide to look through the dustbin in the morning when it was light.

Then another panic. The dustmen were coming round very early tomorrow morning. They had to look through the dustbin that night. Fred went out . . . it was dark, pouring with rain. He couldn't see what he was doing so he dragged the dustbin into their kitchen to search it thoroughly. Unfortunately, in the dark and rain Fred had dragged in the wrong dustbin – the one that belonged to the woman next door.

Meanwhile, the woman next door, hearing a noise, had looked out, heard someone shuffling around, saw that her dustbin was missing, and rang the police who came round seeking some weirdo who was stealing dustbins.

This, of course, led to some amusing complications.

'The Ring' was one of the best episodes. Why? Because so many viewers could identify with the plot.

I'm sure many of them said: 'Something just like that happened to me.'

SO WHAT ARE WE GOING TO WRITE ABOUT THIS WEEK? TRY WORKING FROM THESE ANGLES

1 **Plots that stem directly from your format** – And it's a great help if your format is based on personal experience, you will be able to write what you know about.

2 **Standard subjects that might apply to your format.**

3 **Go through your cast. What do they all want?**

You'll find there's always something to write about. There has to be.

15 Getting along with your director, the actors and the rest of the crew

Here are just some of the team. This is the front page of the camera script of a situation comedy recorded at London Weekend Television Studios. (See page opposite.)

If you write for TV, radio, stage or film, your work only comes to life when it is performed by actors who, in turn, will need the services of technicians and specialists of all types, such as lighting, cameramen etc.

SOME OF THE PEOPLE YOU HAVE TO WORK WITH, AND HOW TO HANDLE THEM
The set designer
When you are writing your script, it's a good idea to make a rough sketch of the living-room, bedroom, shop, workplace or whatever that you are writing about. The set designer should get all the essential information from your script.
It's no use just writing:

THE ACTION TAKES PLACE IN A MIDDLE-CLASS LIVING-ROOM.

There may be many other details important to your script: Is the room in the front of the house? Does it overlook the garden? Does it have a side door? Is it open-plan? etc, etc.
Is there anything special about the room that you need for your comedy? For example: do you need a sofa-bed in which someone could hide? Or in which something could be hidden? If so, it is best to check carefully the type of sofa-bed you want. If necessary, go to a store and have a look at it.
It also helps to get an illustrated catalogue showing the

CAMERA SCRIPT   PROD NO: 0921R

THE RAG TRADE

'THE ANNUAL BALL'

by

RONALD WOLFE & RONALD CHESNEY

PRODUCER/DIRECTOR	WILLIAM G. STEWART
PRODUCTION ASSISTANT	MARION POOLE X 3637
STAGE MANAGER	LAURENCE ROOKE
ASSISTANT STAGE MANAGER	MARY GUNN
COSTUME DESIGNER	BRENDA FOX
MAKE UP	SANDY MACFARLANE
GRAPHICS	CHRIS SHARP
PRODUCTION MANAGER	MIKE MACLOUGHLIN
CASTING	RICHARD PRICE
DESIGNER	ANDREW GARDNER

****

FRIDAY, 7TH JULY   STUDIO 1 (NPD)

        0900-1000 Line Up
        1000-1300 Camera Rehearsal
        1300-1400 Lunch Break
        1400-1600 Camera Rehearsal
        1600-1645 Line Up & Make Up.
        1645-1815 Dress Run
        1815-1915 Dinner Break
        1915-2000 Line Up & Make Up
        2000-2130 VTR
        2130-2330 Strike.

****

SNR. FLOOR MANAGER	LEN SWAINSTON
FLOOR MANAGER	MIKE TOMS
SOUND	KEITH GREEN
GRAMS	ROB LOYD
CAMERAS	JEFF SHEPHERD
VISION MIXER	SANDRA VARDY
LIGHTING DIRECTOR	CHRIS BARTLETT-JUDD
C/OP	PETER RABY
VISION CONTROL SUPERVISOR	TERRY PYRKE
SENIOR ENGINEER	BRIAN LOCKEY
SETTING ASSISTANT	J. WILLIAMS

****

RUNNING TIME: 24'30 (1 commercial break)

exact type of sofa-bed you want for the gag. I believe in the saying, 'One picture is better than ten thousand words.'

If there is anything special you want for a gag – say, a certain type of stepladder, or a certain swivel chair – it is always better to show your designer and props buyer exactly what you want.

A selection of illustrated mail-order catalogues are very useful. Cut out the article you want and show it to the designer and props buyer.

The costume designer

Again, you must clearly describe the clothes your characters are wearing when it's important for the comedy.

You may write:

THE FRONT DOOR. 7.00 A.M.
MICHAEL AND SUSAN DASH OUT.

Now if you want Michael still in his pyjamas and Susan in a nightie, then you must say so. You must write that in your script, otherwise the costume designer might put them in their normal day clothes.

Apart from the actual clothes, there are times when you have to liaise with Wardrobe over a bit of 'business'.

For example – your actor is left alone in a drawing-room in someone's house. He breaks a valuable vase and hurriedly hides the pieces in his trouser pocket on hearing his hostess return. Well, you have to be quite certain that the pockets are big enough to slip in the pieces. The trousers may need some alteration.

In one of our early shows, *The Rag Trade*, we had a bit of business for Sheila Hancock. She was in a panic trying to put on a blouse before the boss came into the workroom. In her hurry, she thrust her head into a sleeve instead of the neck. Her head was stuck in the sleeve so that she looked like a gangster with a stockinged mask. It was funny, but it took some time to get it right. The blouse had to be the right design, the sleeve wide enough, and the material thin enough. In this instance we had to co-operate closely with the costume designer.

Props

In another episode we wanted Barbara Windsor to be chewing bubble-gum and insolently blow out a bubble at the boss. There were problems – no bubble. We had written 'Barbara enters chewing-gum', when we should have written 'Barbara enters chewing bubble-gum'.

Make-up

If that evening, when Michael comes home, we want him to find Susan in the kitchen looking a wreck, with her hair dishevelled, no make-up, etc., then this must be written into the script; otherwise the make-up girls and hairdresser might give Susan the full treatment, so that she looks as though she's just stepped out of a beauty salon. Unless it's clearly written, this is what you might get – and actresses, being actresses, may not object.

The actors

The writer has to learn how to get along with actors, because you can't do the show without them. The actors are the ones who have to face the audience. They have to go out there and do it. So, understandably, they are often worried, anxious and occasionally hysterical. But of course, if they weren't like that, they wouldn't be actors.

One has to be pragmatic. If the actors are good for your script and get the best out of it, then it is worthwhile putting up with a bit of temperament.

There are always tricks you can learn in dealing with actors. It is always a good idea to have your first rehearsal script a little too long, so that when an actor, in a mood, says: 'I can't say that line – it's quite wrong for the character', or, 'It's bad for my image', then it saves much argument by saying: 'That's all right – the script's too long – we can just cut it.'

If an actor insists on altering lines to the detriment of the script, then sometimes a show of strength is necessary. You must remind the actor politely but firmly that there is nothing in his contract that allows him to alter lines, as he does not have script approval. You are pretty safe on these grounds, because only international bankable stars such as Michael Caine, Sean Connery, etc, have script approval clauses.

Usually, this 'shot across the bows' has the desired effect.

The director

A basic problem lies between the writer and the director. The writer has sweated over the script for weeks (or even months if it's for film or stage). The writer knows the script better than the director, but the director has to interpret the script.

The best way for the writer to work with the director is to go through the script carefully line by line to iron out any problems, so that when they go into rehearsal the writer and director are in complete agreement and present a united front to the actors and the rest of the team.

But during rehearsals there will always be things which the writer is not happy about. The correct procedure is for the writer to give his 'notes' privately to the director, who will then give them to the cast.

The writer should always work through the director, as it is confusing to have two bosses and to try and direct the show by committee.

All this may seem reasonable and logical, but if you're on a weekly TV series you're always fighting against time. There's strain and stress, and actors can get difficult under tension. They may want to alter a line or play a scene their way.

In *film-making*, the director does have more chance to manoeuvre. The director can shoot the scene his way, then shoot it the actor's way and, if the director feels like it, the scene shot the actor's way can be left on the cutting-room floor!

The director always has more control in films. I know of an instance when a character actor was specially engaged to do a scene in Cockney, but at the last moment he wanted to do it with a broad Irish accent; to save time, the director let him do this but, when editing the scene, he took out the Irish dialogue and had another actor dub the speeches in Cockney.

But in television you don't have these 'luxuries'. If there is a confrontation, valuable rehearsal time can be lost in argument. Sometimes you have to compromise in order to avoid upsetting the whole production.

There is no point in winning a battle and losing the war. And at that stage of the game the director might be more concerned about keeping his cast happy, than about pacifying the writer.

Whether you like it or not, you are part of a team and you have to learn to accept this, even if it means a certain amount of compromise. If you can't accept it, then you are better off writing novels, short stories, and articles – work that exists in its own right.

The crew you work with are usually very experienced, but on a weekly TV series everyone is under pressure. Remember:

NO ONE KNOWS THE SCRIPT AS WELL AS THE WRITER!

To avoid last minute problems, there is no harm in pointing out parts of the script that might need special attention – as long as this is done tactfully and diplomatically.

One final word. If you expect the other members of the team to do their best, then you too must behave in a professional manner, write workable scripts and deliver on time!

16   *The studio audience*

Are those laughs real?
The questions often asked about studio audiences are: Do you add in the laughs? Dub in some canned laughter?

The official reply from the BBC and major TV companies is usually a self-righteous denial: 'This is against company policy and is strictly forbidden.' However, there are times when dubbing in laughs are justified. Sometimes an actor fluffs or dries on a gag line. It should have got a laugh, but didn't.

At other times, there is a technical breakdown and some lines have to be done again. There are instances in nearly every recording when it's quite fair to add in a laugh.

But officially you are not allowed to add in laughs, so this is what you do. You cheat! And this is how you do it.

There are two easy ways:

1 In the studio, a few minutes before the recording, the 'warm-up' man – or one of the stars of the show – usually tells a few jokes to the audience. These jokes are, of course, tried and trusted and always get big laughs. You record these laughs. You've got them on tape and you can use them to sweeten the actual show when you're editing.

 The important thing is: the laughs you are using come from exactly the same audience as your show, and won't sound as though they're stuck on.

2 Another good way is to plan your script so that it overruns by two or three minutes – no more. This extra bit should consist of a short comedy routine of a few gags which are somewhat extraneous to the plot and easily cut.

 So when you are editing, you can cut out the gags you don't want, but keep the laughs and put them somewhere else in the programme on a line that should have got a laugh but didn't.

I suppose, when you think about it, it's not really cheating. As Sir Humphrey of *Yes Minister* might say: 'It's not dishonest – one is merely rearranging one's resources to achieve maximum results. I mean, it's just good housekeeping.'

Are studio audiences necessary?

Every so often they try a sitcom without an audience and, so far, they haven't been very successful. The opinion is that the viewers like comedies to have laughs in them. TV audiences enjoy comedy more when they hear the laughs.

The Americans, who lead the way with TV comedy, have always taken this laughter business seriously. They have sound engineers, laugh 'doctors' who are expert in dubbing on the laughs.

I know you often see an American show with the caption: 'Recorded before a live audience'. Well, that's true – it is recorded before a live audience – but tampered with afterwards!

I worked at the NBC Studios, Burbank, on the American version of *On the Buses*. We recorded our show before a live audience, and then it was recorded a second time before another live audience. We added the two lots of laughs together and, even then, the show went to the laugh doctors who sweetened and improved reaction as and when necessary.

So when the Americans say a show is recorded before a live audience, they're trying to be a little economical with the truth.

Some American shows are made without an audience, and all the laughter is canned. One of these is *M*A*S*H*. It's filmed on the back lot of Warner Brothers, and the laugh track is put on afterwards.

The odd thing about *M*A*S*H* is that you can buy it with a laugh track or without one. Some of the series shown in England don't have a laugh track, and you'll notice that when delivering a funny line the actors pause for a second or two to allow space for a laugh to be stuck in. If they didn't pause, the laugh would drown the dialogue.

If you write a sitcom to be recorded without an audience, it does affect your dialogue.

For example – let's take a line from *On the Buses*. Arthur, finding Olive tinting her hair, says:

'I didn't know you tinted your hair.'
'Oh, didn't you, Arthur?'
'No, I thought it was natural *mouse*.'

This insult got a laugh. Well, they usually do, and the laugh helps an actor get smoothly into the next line. The laugh is a sort of buffer. But if there was no audience or no laugh, the line would end too abruptly – so to help the dialogue flow more naturally you would add a few more words – something like:

'No, I thought it was natural mouse! However, one lives and learns.'

Personally, I like a studio audience and it's nice for writers who are beginning to know that they can write stuff that gets laughs. But the thing to remember is that when you come to write a film or stage play, there are no laugh tracks in the cinema or theatre. What you don't get, you don't get.

17   *The daily routine*

IT'S ALL IN THE MIND – DON'T PANIC
When you start work, you don't sit down to write a half-hour sitcom – a ninety-minute stage play – or a fifty-minute sketch.

You sit down to write seven or eight pages of your sitcom or play – or ten minutes sketch material.

Think only of the task you can reasonably do that day. Make that your target – achieve that and be happy.

DIVIDE YOUR WORK UP IN DAILY COMPARTMENTS
You probably won't stick to your schedule. Some days you'll do more – sometimes less. But whatever – write something each day.

DEADLINES
A deadline is useful. It helps concentrate the mind and provides the discipline to get you down to work. Many writers like to work to a deadline. A deadline can be an advantage if used properly.

If it takes you about two weeks to write a half-hour script, then it's best to start about three weeks beforehand. But if you start late, and leave yourself just three or four days to meet the deadline, you're likely to panic and bash out what you can in a desperate attempt to fill up the pages.

Some writers might claim they do their best work in a state of panic, up against a deadline. But, in my experience, a script usually reflects the amount of time spent writing it.

WRITER'S BLOCK
There are times when you really get stuck. You struggle for hours, but you can't work out the plot. Or you can't get any further with the dialogue. Your brain seems to be trapped in a single, certain orbit.

If this happens, and actually it happens quite rarely in a busy writer's life, then switch to thinking about something else. Give the mind a break.

Write some of those business letters you keep putting off. Or, better still, write a page or two of that article you promised.

Switching the mind from one problem to another can help.

This process happens frequently when you're doing a crossword puzzle. You get really stumped. You just can't do it. You put it aside and come back to it later to find that the answers to the clues are obvious. You're just amazed you didn't get them the first time.

If your writing has come to a dead stop, then some physical activity might help.

Take a break. Wash the car, or take a sharp walk round the block, or even tear up and down the stairs a few times.

Going to a good movie and getting involved in the plot can sometimes do the trick. Often, when the mind is concentrating on something else, the answer to your script problems just seems to come out of nowhere.

I don't really know how it happens, but I think a comedy writer's brain acts as a computer – always ticking over – trying different permutations and combinations, searching for the right answers. And sometimes those right answers come when we're not screwed up – pressing and straining too much.

A word of warning –

These tricks will help, but don't keep running out for a jog, or dashing off to a movie.

Be honest. Spend sufficient time to justify to yourself that you are genuinely stumped and need to take some action about it.

You must be very conscientious and honest with yourself, otherwise you'll spend all your working hours walking around the block, washing cars, and sitting in the cinema.

18 *Writing with a partner*

WRITING WITH A PARTNER
Should I find myself a partner? Would I really be better off
with a partner?

It's a bit like saying, would I be happier married? The
answer is, it depends on who you marry. It depends on your
personality. You might well be better off single or going solo.

Carla Lane:

> 'I'm not good at collaboration . . . I'm a bit stubborn. I do like
> to use my own phraseology, I can't bear to compromise, I'm
> too dogmatic. I'd sooner write on my own and take the blame
> or the credit.

Carla – creator and writer of shows like *Butterflies* and
Bread – has found that going solo has been best for her.

Men's doubles are common in comedy writing, but in a
successful partnership the resulting work should be much
more than just their combined efforts added together. Ideally,
it should be a better script, and a different script than either
of them could have written individually.

It is not just a case of ONE PLUS ONE EQUALS TWO – but
ONE PLUS ONE EQUALS THREE.

WHAT ARE THE BEST WAYS OF WORKING WITH A PARTNER?
Well, we've all been to a party when the hostess comes over
and says: 'Oh, you are quiet tonight, you must try and liven
up.'

The immediate result is that most of us, instead of livening
up, dry up, retreat, withdraw and shrivel up altogether.

So when you settle down to start writing with a partner,

give the creative juices a chance to flow and avoid being critical.

Too much criticism can be destructive but, on the other hand, some of the ideas and lines suggested may not be very good.

This is what you do
Presumably one of you will be typing or doing the writing as you go along.

Put down everything – Well, everything more or less; the good lines and the 'iffy' lines which need beefing up.

The thing is to **keep going**. Don't be too critical. It's like trying to drive with your brakes on.

Press on to the end of your script. Press on until you've got your first draft finished – however rough.

Make your first draft very long. Write almost twice as much as you need. Then, when you go through it, cutting it down to size – then you can be critical. At that stage you are more critical than creative.

If possible, put that overlong first draft aside for a couple of days. It helps if you can come back fresh to it. It is easier to see what to cut and what to keep – what needs trimming and what needs tightening.

METHODS OF WORKING
Some partners work side by side from the beginning to the end of a script.

John Chapman:

> I wrote *Fresh Fields* for Julia McKenzie and Anton Rogers on my own. The sequel – *French Fields* – I wrote with Ian Davidson. We write facing each other across the desk, thinking up the script line by line. I write it down in longhand and then it is typed up. For me, working with a partner doubles the output, which you need to do because you have to split the fee. But I found it far less stress-making than writing on my own.

Other writers prefer a more hi-tech approach.

Laurence Marks:

Ever since Maurice Gran and I left our day jobs to be professional writers in 1980, we have worked on a word processor.

How do we work physically? When we're working in England, Maurice comes to my place, we sit around discussing the story. It's like a debating society, this could go on for days before we start.

When we are actually writing, Maurice and I take it in turns in the driving seat, i.e. the word processor. We are amending and correcting all the time. It doesn't touch paper until we're happy with what's on the screen, so in reality our first draft is like our twelfth draft.

That's new technology comedy writing I suppose.

As we are amending on the screen all the time, our first draft is very refined, you've got as good as you're going to get.

Working this way there are no rewrites, except in *The New Statesman*, whose process is different to any other because that's a rewrite, and rewrite and rewrite even up to half an hour before the audience come into the studio. This is because the show is very topical.'

Others work together half the time and then alone, and then get back together again.

For example:

If writing a sitcom, the writers get together to hammer out the story line which, let us say, has six scenes.

The partners will have discussed the scenes in detail; then one would go away and write a rough first draft of the first three scenes, and the other writer goes away and writes a rough draft of the last three scenes.

When they get together, they have a rough draft of the whole script. Then slowly they work their way through the whole script from beginning to end, mutually deciding what to keep, what to cut, and what to strengthen.

Some writers find that working together – splitting up to work alone – then getting together for another session is particularly productive.

Two writers working together can sometimes get stuck – they have both been thinking along the same lines. Their minds are in a rut – but if they go off by themselves for some solitary thinking, they often find that when they get together again they have come up with a new angle, a fresh approach that they might not have achieved if they had been working in harness all the time.

WHAT SORT OF PARTNER DO I WANT?

If partners can be chosen or mated by computer, this is the type of information I would feed in.

All writers are not good at all things. Some are better at story lines and construction – some at dialogue, gags or one-liners.

If both partners are gag men, you might get a very 'gaggy' script with a weak story line.

If they're both good at story lines, you might get a good story but not enough actual laugh lines.

In partnership, it helps if one is better at construction and the other better at dialogue. Ideally, their talents should be somewhat different – though of course there will be some overlap.

Their personalities should also be somewhat different. In many successful writing partnerships, one partner is often more outgoing than the other. And you frequently find that one is better at money-matters and contracts, while the other is better at handling artists, and so forth; and you realize that between them you find a whole range of skills which you rarely find in just one person.

As partners have to work together without too many distractions, it is most desirable that each partner has a stable uncomplicated private life.

There is nothing worse for two writers, battling to finish a script, than to have non-stop phone calls from jealous, suspicious husbands or wives, boyfriends or girlfriends, assorted lovers, or one-night stands demanding a 'commitment'.

Writing comedy is a tough business. There are enough problems – you don't need any extra hassle!

How Andy Hamilton and Guy Jenkin write *Drop the Dead Donkey*

Andy Hamilton:

Because of the structure of *Donkey*, you've got to have a good central plot and then you've got to have interesting subplots. We've got eight characters and we've got to keep them involved. So we start by having some big sessions talking about the main plots, you know, like someone getting divorced or someone with a fear of dying – something substantial. We get ten or eleven ideas for main plots and then we get ideas for reasonably chunky subplots – like Joy appearing on *Gladiators* – and then we have another column, like junior subplots – just runners.

We talk through the episodes and, of course, while doing this a lot of dialogue happens as we chat our way through. We make notes and we keep on till we get a reasonable structure to all of the episodes and then we decide who will do the first draft of that episode. Now, if we're lucky, an awful lot of dialogue has cropped up while we were talking about the episode, so it can be just a question of writing it out. Sometimes there is only just a thread that you haven't really talked about in detail.

We do an equal amount of first drafts and then after that we do the second, third and fourth drafts together. Sometimes if there are problems we do a fifth draft. We do it across a desk. We don't have a word processor – we work by hand. If we hit a problem scene, one of us may take it away to get it into a better shape. But fundamentally, the rewrite is done together and we work on the premise that each line has got to get past both of us. If one of us is not happy, then that line has to come out. Usually, we have a series of twelve episodes. So we start with the main plots for at least fourteen episodes so that we have some in hand in case things don't quite work out.

But unlike some teams, Hamilton and Jenkin don't write everything together:

We do different things on our own. We're quite promiscuous really. We find doing different things on our own stops us getting stale. We enjoy it when we get back together. I recently wrote a television comedy drama *Eleven v. Eleven* which I also directed and Guy Jenkin wrote the much-acclaimed television comedy play *A Very Open Prison*.

TEAM WRITING

But there is a limit to the output even of two experienced writing partners.

Laurence Marks:

> We had worked in the States and saw the advantage of the American system of team-writing. It allows you much longer runs. We always wanted to try this, and started with one series of *Birds of a Feather* over here. We recruited by and large some very inexperienced writers. We thought those with potential would be better off coming into an existing hit show. There could be fourteen people round the table discussing ideas and possible story lines. Individuals or partners would then take an idea each, go away and develop it into scene breakdowns.
>
> Some of us would meet up again – there could be maybe eight people discussing the one story line and inevitably strengthening it.
>
> The writer who created that story line would go away and write his first draft, then Maurice and I would work closely with the writer to produce the final draft.
>
> Some writers develop better and sooner than others. Our intent is that the writers who had proved themselves would go off and create their own series, and the writers who were still down the learning curve would contribute to these new series.
>
> I always describe it as like the Liverpool football club youth policies. Get good youth at your base, teach them through other people's series, and eventually they'll be able to create a series of their own . . . As long as we keep recruiting talent, we hope never to run out of series and writers.

Beryl Vertue:

> I personally don't like working that way. I prefer the main writer, the creator, to shine. In drama I think team writing can work, but I am not sure about comedy, well not here, not in this country.

How has the team-writing experiment by Alomo been working out?

Micheál Jacob, script executive Alomo TV, producer of *Birds
of a Feather*:

> In retrospect, it was felt that it was difficult to integrate a
> number of writers without experience of the show, so an
> informal rule of one or at the most two new writers per series
> has been adopted.
>
> From the series 2 experience Alomo found Sue Teddern,
> who had written many episodes of *Birds*, then went on to
> other projects. A pair of new writers, Coombes and Robinson,
> went on to write several episodes of *Lovejoy*, and other
> comedy dramas.
>
> Other writers from early days to have continued their
> involvement with *Birds* and other shows are Gary Lawson and
> John Phelps, Geoff Rowley and Peter Tilbury. All had previ-
> ously written broadcast work, and Peter Tilbury had created
> and written *Shelley*.
>
> Whether the writer is new, or hugely experienced (like Peter
> Tilbury) we require a storyline before a first draft, and we do
> notes at each stage of the process.
>
> Our policy is to leave people alone to get on with it, while
> always being available to help if a writer is having particular
> problems. It is stating the obvious to say that the process is
> generally more angst-free with experienced writers.

19   What shall it be? Radio, television, films or stage?

They all have their pros and cons, advantages and disadvantages for the writer.

RADIO
The absolute freedom of it is appealing to the comedy writer. You don't have to worry about sets, costume changes, make-up or wigs. You can be anywhere so easily.

If you are writing a sitcom for radio, you can go to as many different places as you like. A few words of dialogue, a sound effect, sometimes a snatch of music, and that's it! you're there! You've established a mental picture.

On radio – obviously – the actors have only their voices to create their characters. We are lucky in England that a person's speech tells so much about them (little has altered since *Pygmalion*), and there are also regional accents and, of course, foreign accents. All of these help to create the right mental picture in the listener's mind.

The writer of a sitcom for radio has enormous scope and, in sketch writing, imagination can really run riot. The only restriction is the limit of your imagination.

You can have one character at the top of Mount Everest speaking to another character in a submarine on the ocean bed. You can go forwards in time – backwards in time – going anywhere, doing anything.

Radio lends itself to fantasy. A good example of this was a sketch written by Eric Sykes in the heyday of radio:

Eric had all the well-known statues in London coming to life and meeting up late at night:

116

BOADICEA DRIVING HER CHARIOT DOWN TO TRAFALGAR
SQUARE TO HAVE A CHAT WITH LORD NELSON, etc etc.

And, of course, every possibility of radio writing was
explored by Spike Milligan and the Goons.

Radio is still very much a writer's medium.

One advantage is that the cast don't have to learn the
script. They can read it. So the rehearsal time is short. The
cast only have to meet a few hours before the recording.
There are usually two run-throughs and then the audience
come into the studio. The recording is done – and that's it.

The radio writer has an easier time – less stress, but
unfortunately less money than in television.

TELEVISION

The usual sitcom is recorded in a television studio before an
audience of about two hundred.

The writer is restricted by the number of sets. **There is
room for only two or three major sets facing the audience.** It
is expected that the action of the script takes place mostly in
these sets.

If the writer needs some external scenes – the outside of the
house – the car going down the street, etc., this will be
pre-recorded by a film unit, then edited into the show at the
right place.

In a television series, the actors have not only to learn their
lines, but also the moves, and have to worry about being on
the right mark for the cameras.

When the director wants a nice close-up for a reaction
shot, the actor has to be in exactly the right place at the right
time, and saying the right line.

It is a great help if the writer uses the same sets in each
episode as much as possible. If the actors and director are
used to the set and are familiar with it, there is less time
wasted worrying about the moves.

The actors can then concentrate more on delivering their
lines and, hopefully, getting more laughs from your script.

The other advantage of using the same sets is that the
writer can visualize the script as he writes it. He knows the
layout – he knows where the actors sit – he can write more
polished script that will need less alteration in rehearsal.

Viewers also like to see their favourite characters in a familiar setting; it makes them feel part of the family.

The top American sitcoms nearly always take place in the same sets week after week. *The Cosby Show, The Golden Girls* and, of course, *Cheers*. Regular viewers not only know the set in *Cheers*, they also know the place at the bar counter where each of the regulars sit. After a few weeks, you feel as though you are in the bar with them.

On a television series, the cast are together at least six hours a day for six days a week. They go over the script again and again and again. Not surprisingly, after about the fourth day, they sometimes feel that it's not very funny.

The lines they thought were quite brilliant at the first read-through now seem most unfunny. This is not surprising, as they've probably said them about fifty times. They start to lose confidence in the script; they over-analyse it – want to alter things – take out essential plot lines. They think that they're improving the script, but usually they're making it worse.

The writer's job is to pop into rehearsal every other day and tactfully take out the 'improvements'. It is not easy, but the comedy writer has to fight for and protect his laughs.

Rehearsals are held in an outside rehearsal room. On the day of recording, the show goes into the proper studio and then the cast see the set for the first time.

If the sets are the same ones that are used each week – the living-room, the office, the workroom or the bar – then the cast feel more at home, and the director and camera crew are also familiar with the set.

This means that most of the moves, the action and the camera shots, will work. The technical run-through will go smoothly; there will be less things to go wrong, less problems to sort out and, hopefully, a better, slicker, well-rehearsed show.

There is far more stress and tension when writing for television than when working in radio.

On the other hand, television has more impact and, even after only a few episodes, a new writer will be noticed.

It can be almost instant success, bringing fame, acclaim and money. The rate for television scripts is about ten times that for radio.

But television is much more demanding. You need stamina as well as talent, but as the saying goes – 'If you can't take the heat, keep out of the kitchen'.

FILMS

Forget about Hollywood – forget about megabucks for the time being. Let's be practical. If you're a comedy writer working in England, the only comedy film script you're likely to be asked to write – at least in the first instance – will be for a low-budget film. That is, a film which will cover its costs when shown in the UK.

The writer of a British comedy film has to be very concerned with the budget. Your script may be brilliant, but if it's going to cost at least two million pounds to make, and the budget is one million, it is most unlikely that the film will be made.

To write a funny script is not enough. You have to use your skill and ingenuity to see that not a penny of the budget is wasted. You want to see every penny up there on the screen.

The film script is a sequence of scenes. Each scene is an INTERIOR, i.e. shot in the studio; or an EXTERIOR, i.e. shot on location.

A good comedy film should have strong visual gags, and plenty of action. These are usually exterior shots on location, and expensive. The interior shots in the studio are cheaper, so your script should have a balance – say, half interior and half exterior.

Interiors, by comparison, are less exciting. When you're writing it is bad policy to have one interior after another after another. It can be dreary. Try to construct your script so that a quietish interior is followed by an exciting exterior.

Space out your big visual laughs so that they are dotted evenly throughout the film. This keeps the laughs bubbling over and the audience happy, even through the quieter bits.

I know we all want a big, funny ending, but it's no use keeping all your big exterior shots till the end of the film. You may have lost your audience by then.

Most television writers have found that they can make the transition to film-writing with reasonable ease. You soon find out what works and what doesn't.

In a sitcom, most of the scenes are interiors, with your characters sitting around with long stretches of dialogue.

In the cinema, these scenes seem slow. The film loses pace. But exteriors are expensive. Going on location is like a small army on the move. The cameras, lighting generators, mobile dressing rooms, canteen, technicians, actors – they all have to be transported. It's costly.

Locations

Don't write a story that needs locations at places like Dover Harbour, then Edinburgh, then North Wales or Cornwall. The film unit will waste time and money on the motorways, getting from one location to another.

Plan your script and story line so that most of the exterior work can be done in one location. Choose that location carefully. Pick one that gives you plenty of variety – e.g. a London Docklands Development area.

> Think of it – **The Docklands**; luxury penthouses, warehouse conversions, old working-class homes; pubs; health clubs; factories; offices; and, of course, the river; shipping; boats. All within one location. All the 'set-ups' are within easy reach of each other.

Set-ups

Again, make sure you get maximum value out of each set-up. Don't get the lighting and camera set up in position for just one laugh. Aim at getting three laughs out of each set-up. If you can think of only one – then you might consider cutting it and finding another set-up that will be more fruitful.

Films are, of course, shot out of sequence. If there is a scene in a hotel lobby at the beginning, middle and, again, at the end of the film, then those scenes will all be filmed at the same time on one day.

This system can be exploited by the writer. You might consider writing up the hotel manager's part into a comedy cameo, and cast a well-known actor.

Such an actor will not come cheap, but you will only be employing him for one day or two. But he will be popping up at intervals throughout the film, giving it a little boost here and there.

At first, you may find all this worry about budget stifling to the creative juices. But learning to write within the restrictions of the budget is part of the job.

Remember, if your film is funny, on budget, and makes a profit, then you have more chance of being asked to write another one. Which may lead to Hollywood and megabucks!

STAGE

Going from radio to television, and then to films is something that most writers can take in their stride. But writers embarking on their first stage play soon find that there's some hard thinking to do.

A stage comedy will take place in one set, or a composite set; it usually has two acts and one interval.

You plot out your scenes like this:

ACT ONE, SCENE ONE. HOTEL ROOM.
MICHAEL AND SUSAN ENTER WITH THEIR LUGGAGE.

SCENE TWO. FOUR HOURS LATER
MICHAEL AND SUSAN HAVE UNPACKED AND ARE IN BED. IT IS DARK. THEY HEAR A NOISE.

Then it suddenly dawns on you. What is going to be happening on the stage between Scene One and Scene Two.

In TV and on film, you stop recording or filming. The actors change their costumes. The set is altered. You don't have to worry about time lapses or costume changes.

Suddenly, the film and TV writer is aware of problems he hasn't had to deal with before.

A time lapse on the stage is not too bad. This can be achieved by lighting, going almost to black for a few seconds.

But what about costume changes?

Michael and Susan are on stage. If they go off for a quick costume change they'll leave an empty stage. This is where you use other characters or, if necessary, create other characters to help the changes, and go from Scene One to Scene Two like this:

TOWARDS THE END OF SCENE ONE, THE HOTEL MANAGER AND MAID ENTER. (You write a reason for them to enter.)
MICHAEL AND SUSAN GO OFF. (You write a reason for this.)
THERE ARE TWO OR THREE MINUTES DIALOGUE BETWEEN THE

HOTEL MANAGER AND THE MAID (POSSIBLY PART OF A SUB-PLOT).
THEN SCENE ONE ENDS WITH A FIVE-SECOND BLACKOUT.
LIGHTS UP AGAIN.
IT IS NOW SCENE TWO. FOUR HOURS LATER.
MICHAEL AND SUSAN ARE IN BED. (Having made a quick change.)

Apart from the time lapse and costume change, the writer has to find reasons for getting actors on and off stage as and when he wants them.

These movements can be most complicated, and the stage play can be mind-boggling at first.

From sitcom to stage

John Chapman (co-writer with Ray Cooney of such farces as *Move Over Mrs Markham* and *Not Now Darling*):

> There is a useful definition. **Situation comedy** is unreal people in real situations, whereas **farce** is real people in unreal situations.
>
> The story line in a sitcom can be trivial . . . giving up smoking . . . forgetting a birthday.
>
> The farce needs a strong overpowering story. A story which, if treated a different way, could be a drama. This strong story is vital to sustain the two hours needed for the average farce.
>
> In a farce, every character must complicate the plot in some way, and have a strong angle. There must be plenty of twists and turns.
>
> In a sitcom such as *The Golden Girls*, usually three out of the four girls only have little conflicts between them . . . different attitudes to each other, but face the main problem in harness.
>
> Ideally, the story should take place over a short period of time, a few days . . . but, if possible, over a period of just two or three hours. To sum up – situation comedy is a storm in a teacup, a play is the storm.

Alan Plater:

> The main difference between television and stage is what you can expect of your audience. The theatre is an empty space and you will fill it with your imagination. You also rely on

your audience to help you. The theatre is tough because it has fewer limitations. I think there is a sort of equation which says the more limitations there are, the easier they are to do.

In a half-hour sitcom, certain things are laid down. You have to do it using about four sets, and that's it. You have to do it more or less continuously, and that determines the structure of the story.

The theatre is toughest because the possibilities are greatest.

However, a stage production does have certain advantages over TV. There is a longer rehearsal time and the luxury of trying out the play on tour or with previews.

On a try-out tour, the writer gets a chance to judge audience reaction and then make alterations. There can be rewrites; different lines tried out. Even whole scenes taken out and new ones put in.

There can be changes not only in the script, but also in the cast.

The audience

When writing for the stage, be aware of the theatre audience. On TV, you have to grab your audience in the first minute or two, and hold them. In the theatre, the opening can be more laid back.

The audience is settling down; some people may just be coming in. They need time to relax.

Start simply, without too many characters on stage, and without immediate dialogue. Have the characters doing some simple action – like pouring a drink, or tidying up. This gives the audience a chance to examine the set and start to focus on what is about to happen.

It is not like TV. The audience is not going to switch off. They have paid their money and they are not going to walk out (well, at least not until the interval!). And, unlike the TV audience with the distractions of the home, the theatre audience will make an effort to concentrate.

The interval in a stage play should be treated like the commercial break in a TV sitcom.

The first act must end with some good, strong laughs and a bit of a cliffhanger; a plot twist. You want your audience to go out for the interval laughing, chuckling, happy, discussing the plot and happily anticipating the second act.

After the interval is just like after the commercial break; the same technique. Remind the audience of the plot, and then some good, strong gags to get them back in the mood again.

RADIO, TV, FILMS OR STAGE – FOUR POSSIBILITIES
In an ideal world, a writer should be trying his luck in every field. This isn't always possible, but it's a good idea to try your luck in at least two of them.

Alan Plater:

> It pays to have many irons in the fire, and to work in at least two branches of the media.
> *Peggy For You* was written on spec and very quickly. Peggy Ramsay was the most amazing woman I ever knew, outside of the family. The form of the play is a day in the life of her office in the late 1960s. I wrote the first draft in a couple of weeks or so. Second draft about the same. That version, with tweaks in the rehearsal room, was the one we did at Hampstead. We took out some of the improvements for the West End and the tour!
> *Peggy For You* was like a dream – written quickly and produced quickly. Not so *Last of the Blonde Bombshells*. This had a twelve-year history. Originally written as an hour-long television piece for a six-part series that never happened, I later expanded it into a spec screenplay for a feature film that almost happened, but not quite. By that time we had commitments from Judi Dench and Ian Holm and this obviously eased the way on to television, though it wasn't as smooth a passage as you might expect. Judi and Ian were totally loyal to the project from day one. Over the entire life of the project I did about fourteen versions!

Even a writer like Alan Plater has to work on spec sometimes. And learn above all that you must persevere.

20 *Stand-up comedy*

Writing for stand-up comics – how do you start?
First of all you pick a subject or subjects, or you might be
given a subject.

Most stand-up comics of the Jasper Carrott or Dave Allen
type, usually stay on one subject – get as much fun as possible
out of that subject before moving on.

Their subject might be advertising, do it yourself, going on
holiday, etc.

Say the subject decided on is going on holiday. The first
stage is 'Association'. Make a list of everything associated
with holidays:

Passports
Packing
Getting to the airport
The flight
The hotel
The food . . . The other guests . . . etc., etc.

In fact, as many associations as you can.

This list may run to forty or fifty words, maybe more
depending on the length of the routine.

The next stage is to try and work out a gag or two for each
word on the list.

Let's think about the 'plane – it might be an old charter
'plane:

The 'plane was so old it had a rear gunner at the back.

Or there might be an angle on the different airlines:

Have you ever travelled El Al? What salesmanship . . . the Captain comes round with duty frees . . . during take-off.

Or think about the airport . . . of all the facilities. Be a little curious about them. I am sure that approach inspired a really wild gag from Mel Brooks:

You know, at every big airport they have a chaplain . . . you know what he does? . . . shouts prayers at crashing pilots.

When you have sufficient gags you routine them . . . put them in some sort of order so that the continuity flows . . . getting you easily from one gag to another.

WRITING GAG ROUTINES IS HARD WORK – A HARD SLOG: It is easier if the person you are writing for has a definite attitude – a recognizable style – in fact, a character.

The character stand-up comic
Although she is a fine actress, Beryl Reid first came to fame as Monica – the awful schoolgirl.

Monica was based on one of the scruffy outrageous schoolgirls of St Trinians, created by Ronald Searle.

Beryl did a stand-up routine dressed in a very stained and torn schoolgirl uniform, quite revolting in every way.

One of the routines I wrote for her started like this:

We had a simply scrumptious time in the dormitory last night. I handed round cigarettes . . . I rolled them myself . . . brown paper and bed fluff. Then we made ourselves some mushrooms on toast . . . we found the mushrooms growing out of the wall. I suppose our dormy is in a bit of a mess. The other day our Headmistress Miss Oglethorpe came in and said, she said, "Monica, there are things under your bed that David Attenborough could not identify". She's always telling me off for being scruffy. Well, I can't be bothered with laundry and all that . . . that's why I wear a string vest . . . you don't have to wash it . . . you wait till the holes clog up, then poke them out with a pencil.

Not all stand-up comics have gag routines
Shelly Berman – a most successful American comedian – had an attitude. He was a man aggrieved by a slipshod world.

He had his own special brand of humour. One of his routines went something like this:

Sitting on a stool, with his left hand forming a telephone, he was making a call to Macey's – the famous department store in New York:

Hello, is that Macey's? Well listen, operator . . . I am in the office block across the street and there's a man on a ledge outside your building . . . he's going to jump and . . . what floor? How do I know what floor? Oh, alright . . . put me through. Who's that . . . information? Look, there's a man perched on a ledge and he's going to jump . . . I don't know what floor . . . the fourteenth or fifteenth . . . does it matter whether it is soft furnishings or bathroom accessories or lampshades? Do something. Put me on to someone . . . alright. Who's that . . . complaints? No, I am not an account customer . . .

So he was transferred from one department to another – the staff more concerned with passing the buck than the potential suicide.

The beauty of this sort of routine is that you don't have to bash out gag after gag – you just need the one idea. In a way, it's like writing a sketch . . . once you get the idea, you're away.

What Shelly Berman was really doing was describing a sketch to the audience . . . telling them a story – creating a mental picture.

STAND-UP COMICS NEED A LOT OF MATERIAL

A comic standing alone on stage in the theatre or cabaret has to dominate his or her audience. Especially in the theatre or cabaret, he has to be in charge, to have control over an audience, and this can only be done with the right material.

A good comic will like to get at least two, maybe three laughs a minute. This means a lot of gags.

In an earlier chapter there were some examples of reversals, type gags, exaggerations, comparisons, switching, surprise.

You can't write gags by formula, but it is useful to know

the different types. It is a help to know the type of line you are aiming for when you are writing. Here are a few examples:

Direct insult (Groucho-Marx style)

To the woman who had been on a diet: You say you lost seven pounds? You haven't lost it. It's right behind you.

Groucho on age: You say you're just approaching sixty? From which direction?

Indirect insult

Did you find my house alright?
Sure – only an idiot could get lost.
You must have had a terrible journey.

False logic

She said those pills I keep popping were habit-forming. She's crazy, they're not habit-forming. I ought to know, I've been taking them for years.
OR:
He went to medical school. He wanted to be a brain surgeon, but they said he wasn't tall enough . . . so they made him a gynaecologist.

Combination

The chiropodist who took up palmistry. Now he reads feet.

Malaprops

She's very good at language. She's fluid in French . . . she's what you call bifocal.

Twisting old jokes

There used to be a joke about a woman going into a ladies' hairdresser:

Which girl does the shampooing?
The one with the clean hands.

I wrote a restaurant sketch, where a waiter, serving a brimming bowl of soup, came out holding the bowl of soup. This time the joke was:

Which waiter serves the soup?
The one with the clean thumbs.

SOME JOKES CAN BE UPDATED:
In the 1950s the Germans brought out a new baby car . . . a two-seater with a plastic hood called a bubble car.
The topical joke was:

They asked me if I wanted to buy a bubble car. I said I'm buying two . . . one for each foot.

In the 1960s the first mini came out. The joke was then:

Are you buying a mini?
I'm buying two . . . one for each foot.

In the 1980s Clive Sinclair – the inventor – launched a little town runabout, the all-electric Sinclair. The joke was:

Are you buying one of those Sinclair runabouts?
I'm buying two . . . YES, THAT'S RIGHT . . .

I wonder where and when we're going to hear it next?

ARE THERE ANY NEW JOKES?
Well, there are always new things to write about.
One of our new young comedians, Jack Dee has developed some very funny and original material based on the modern electronic gadgets we surround ourselves with:

. . . I've got trouble with my ansaphone . . . my ansaphone has got an attitude problem. I came in the other night, switched on, it went: 'Erm . . . let me think now . . . oh, erm, yes, there was something . . . can't remember what he said . . . anyway, didn't sound important . . . he sounded really boring . . . anyway, it was about three days ago . . .'
Another time I set my video to record that film *Out of Africa*. I switched on to enjoy the film. All I got was: 'Erm . . .

about that film . . . I'll tell you about it . . . It was really dreary
. . . Meryl Streep sitting in that tent . . . sobbing her heart out
. . . wondering if she'd got clap . . . I switched over to the
other channel to watch football . . .'

With this refreshing approach, Jack Dee was the surprise hit
of the stand-up comedy season, Queens Theatre London in
the autumn of 1990.

**Writing for stand-up comics is one of the hardest and least
rewarding jobs in the business**
Why do it?
It is one of the ways to break into the business. When you're
starting out it's easier to sell a gag routine than a sitcom.

If you write for an up-and-coming comic he may open a
few doors for you as he goes up in the world.

If not, whatever happens, the experience is invaluable.

21 *Women in comedy*

Women have always featured strongly in television comedy, but the writers have nearly always been men.

Prunella Scales' first TV success was in *Marriage Lines*, co-starring Richard Briers, and written by Richard Waring.

Felicity Kendal and Penelope Keith each scored a great personal success in *The Good Life*, written by John Esmonde and Bob Larbey, and, again, Penelope Keith was the star of *To the Manor Born* written by Peter Spence.

No wonder that most male writers thought they could write quite adequately for women, but that was until Carla Lane came along.

Carla's scripts for *Butterflies* — first screened in 1978 — explored fresh territory. This was comedy with a sensitive theme.

In this series Rhea, played by Wendy Craig, was a housewife who loves her two sons and her husband, but is bored stiff with looking after them.

She is attracted to a man she accidentally met in a coffee shop, after flicking ash into his trifle.

Here is an extract from the scene in which she is nonchalantly trying to slip away from the family in the hope of meeting him again.

Her husband and her two sons are finishing their lunch. Rhea is anxious to get out:

> . . . I am in a hurry to get to the shops . . . the percolator is on . . . the coffee will be ready in five minutes, the cups are hanging in the kitchen, and the kitchen is due north. If one of you should get lost en route, the other two can form a search party.

One of her sons says:

That's alright mum, go right out and enjoy yourself.

Rhea replies:

Enjoy myself??? Who said anything about enjoying myself? I never enjoy myself. How dare you accuse me of enjoying myself. I devote my entire existence to this family ship. I am the cook, the laundry maid, and the captain. I hoist the sails, scrub the decks and ding the dongs, and when you lot are sprawled in front of the telly enjoying yourselves, you will find me slumped over the helm composing tomorrow's dinner.

Carla writes entirely from a woman's point of view.

WHY AREN'T THERE MORE WOMEN WRITING COMEDY?
Carla Lane:

There doesn't seem to be many. I don't really know why that is. More women write drama. I suppose in a way I also write drama, although it gets a laugh . . . what I mean is, I don't really write jokes . . . or what I call silly lines.

Maybe women don't write comedy because it's still looked down upon. When I tell people I'm a writer, they ask what I write. When I say 'comedy', they say, 'oh' – a bit disappointed.

Last year I wrote two little plays. Everyone seemed impressed . . . I had status. I thought, 'Oh, suddenly I'm a writer.'

COMEDY HAS ALWAYS BEEN SEXIST
In stand-up comedy, the jokes and the insult routines were about the wife . . . the mother-in-law . . . The gags were sexist . . . It was always, *she* was so ugly that . . . she was *so* fat that . . . It was always '*she*' and not '*he*'.

Then along came women like Victoria Wood, and the women started getting their own back on the men for years of insults. Most of them do gags against their husbands and boyfriends, and get many laughs describing the inadequacies of their love-making.

Victoria Wood – who has great fun describing the inadequacies of her boyfriend – has a marvellous gag:

> I had a terrible time with my first boyfriend. He had a sex manual – but he was dyslectic. I was lying in bed, and he was looking for my vinegar.

Unlike Carla, Victoria Wood first became noticed as a playwright. She had two stage plays performed, and three television plays, between 1978 and 1981 – an impressive start as she was then only in her mid-twenties.

More and more comediennes have come on to the scene – French and Saunders, Ruby Wax, Helen Lederer, and many others.

But so far, not many writers. These women all write comedy, but they write for themselves, and perform it themselves.

HOW DIFFICULT IS IT FOR A WOMAN WRITER TO BREAK IN?
Sue Teddern was a journalist and now writes sitcom and comedy-drama full-time:

> I think I'm funny . . . lots of my articles were funny . . . so I thought, why not exploit it?
>
> A few years ago I met Marks and Gran when I interviewed them for *The Guardian*. I sent them an idea I had for a sitcom. They liked it, and asked if I'd like to write for *Birds of a Feather*.
>
> I think that there are so few women writing comedy because there are very few women in a position of power to commission comedy.
>
> There is a gulf to be breached . . . a gulf of understanding, because women write comedy in a different way.
>
> Instead of trying to copy men and not succeeding, they should celebrate what they want to do and do it well.
>
> Carla Lane has found a different way of doing comedy. While the style is unique to her, I think it is a slightly reflective style that a lot of women are very good at.
>
> Sometimes you write something which other women

appreciate, but which is lost on men.

For too long, women have been portrayed as a 'bimbo' or a 'battle-axe', with no light or shade.

The role of women has changed in the outside world, and therefore it must change in contemporary comedy.

I am sure that there will be many more women writers, because once you see other women doing it you think, 'Oh, I can do that too'.

If you make up your mind that you are going to do it, people will recognize your determination. It's a state of mind. Your approach to people must be that you mean business.

I enjoy working on the *Birds* writing team. It's been my sitcom apprenticeship. I just wish there were more opportunities for new writers – both men and women – to benefit from the team-writing experience.

How did Lucy Flannery break in?

My first credits were for writing some episodes of *Close to Home* – a London Weekend sitcom starring Richard O'Sullivan of *Man About the House* fame. I'd sent a script to Robin Carr, the executive producer: he thought it showed promise and asked me to join the writing team. I was – as usual – the only woman on it.

But I had been writing for some time. I was working in local government, but I chucked it to be a writer. You have to take a risk . . . bite the bullet. You can be too busy earning a living to do anything else.

I was inspired by the comedy in the early eighties . . . by Victoria Wood, *The Young Ones*, *Girls on Top*, French and Saunders. It became quite a hip thing to do – quite trendy to be a comedy writer. I think that there are a lot of women writing, but very few women are actually commissioned or sell their work. This is because most people who commission are men: they don't really understand that women do approach comedy in a slightly different way.

Any hints or tips?

Be true to yourself. It's no use sitting down and thinking up a format and saying . . . 'because this TV company did this, and another TV company did that, I should do something similar'. It's not my cup of tea . . . it's not my style, but nevertheless I'll do it.

This never works. You really have got to write what you believe in. I also believe that the audience is far more intelligent than they are given credit for. No one can teach you how to write comedy, but they can teach you how to write better. The problem is persuading a producer that it's funny. I'm interested in writing good comedy – male or female.

To me, situation comedy is character comedy.

Good characterizations are my first love. I don't start by saying, 'What am I going to write a sitcom about? Shall I write one that takes place in a florist or a chemist shop?' There's nothing intrinsically funny about that. It is the people who are in it – the characters. If you create good characters, they can be funny anywhere.

Have plenty of irons in the fire.

In the beginning, you have one brilliant idea; you pour everything into it. All your energy. You send it off and wait, and it's rejected. You're shattered. You think it's the end. You must have plenty of projects on the boil. Don't concentrate too much on one market.

BUT WOMEN ARE SLOWLY MOVING INTO POSITIONS OF POWER

Today there are more women producers and directors. There's Mandy Fletcher – a much sought-after, award-winning director, who has been directing episodes of *Blackadder* for BBC TV, and *Desmond's* – a Humphrey Barclay Production for Channel Four.

When I was made a director at the BBC, the Head of Comedy, John Howard Davies, kissed me, saying, 'You're the first comedy director I've ever kissed'. I said, 'I'm not surprised. I'm the first woman. All the rest were men'.

Did you have any problems?

No – not at all; not with the actors or the crews. There was never any anti-feeling. My background as an actress must have helped, and I had also directed in the theatre.

Being the first woman comedy director at the BBC was a bit

of a fluke. I was in the right place at the right time. I started in television as an assistant floor manager, and worked my way up to be a production manager. I was working for Sid Lotterby who was then producer/director of *Butterflies*. He gave me an opportunity to direct a couple of episodes. The moment Michael Grade became controller and said there weren't enough woman directors, the head of comedy triumphantly announced: 'We've got a woman; a production manager who has actually directed two episodes. I think we'll promote her.'

Yes, I was in the right place. I was lucky. I knew it. I made up my mind not to blow it.

I was the only girl at all those production meetings. I remember sitting there in a purple flying suit and green sneakers, and they were all in their navy blazers with brass buttons, and dark blue suits. After a while I felt I didn't fit in, and left to freelance, doing shows like *Desmond's*.

I like directing comedy. I have a respect for the writers. Writing comedy is difficult, and I admire anyone who can do it.

We need some new young comedy writers, and they need the experience to learn their craft. I mean, just take the first episode of a series . . . just think of the problems. So many things to get into twenty-five minutes . . . introduce all the characters, tell a story and be funny.

Beryl Vertue, though practically unknown to the public, is one of the most experienced women in television production. Her company Hartswood Films produces such shows as *Men Behaving Badly*, *Is It Legal?*, and *My Good Friend*, starring George Cole.

Though not a writer herself, Beryl knows about writing, and cares about writers:

Over the years I've learnt to be a good editor, and how to get along with writers. I've represented writers as an agent and I know the agony of sitting there just looking at a blank page. When a script comes in, I ring them very quickly even to say I haven't read it yet. Because sometimes I'm not in the mood for it or I may feel a bit tired.

When I read a script I like to see the picture. There's one tip to a writer I would like to say. Try and pretend you are the director. Try and see the picture you are trying to create and not just the words. Also if you sometimes have a scene that doesn't seem to be working, keep thinking of the characters in that scene. If you were the actor playing those parts, what would you be doing ... what would you be saying?

Why aren't there many more women comedy writers?

It does seem that most of the women writers are drama writers. The women who can write good comedy material, are usually artistes themselves working their own material. I don't know why this is. But it's a fact ... like most of the casting directors are women. It is also a fact that more and more women seem to be producing and directing comedy. So maybe there will be more openings on the production side.

What do you think is a good way into this business?

I used to say learn shorthand typing, or something like that. Though of course nowadays I'd say learn how to work a computer. Whatever skill you have or acquire find a reason to get into a studio or production office. Get hired for something and go from there. You can't expect to waltz into a place and get a job as a producer or director. You don't know anything yet. But it is important to be of help, to work hard. I am sure you don't have to be there very long before someone says, she's bright, and you can get a chance to move on. Make yourself useful – it is surprising where you can end up.

I started when I was sixteen. I was a secretary at Associated London Scripts. Among the writers there were Galton and Simpson, and Johnny Speight. I became involved in sorting out contracts and discussing fees. Then one day someone said to me, 'How long have you been an agent?' And then I realized that's what I had become. I enjoyed being an agent. I was fortunate enough to be with some very good people. The next move was into production.

ANOTHER WOMAN AMONGST THE FIRST OF THE FEW IS SUSAN BELBIN
Susan Belbin – who has directed some episodes of *'Allo 'Allo*, and produced and directed the hugely successful *One Foot in the Grave* which received a BAFTA nomination after only its first series.

Susan worked in the theatre, joined the BBC many years ago, and was determined and ambitious:

I always thought I'd be a producer, although there weren't many women around then.

I think women were brainwashed into thinking that they couldn't do certain jobs, couldn't rise higher than a secretary or production assistant. They seemed to accept this.

They were 'conned' again when some of them wanted to join the camera crew. They were told they weren't strong enough to handle the equipment. Then it was pointed out that if a young mother could often lug two kids, a pusher, and bags of shopping on and off buses, in and out of cars, up and down stairs, then a woman was quite strong enough to push a camera around the studio.

About women not wanting to write stuff to please a male director, I don't think it matters. You must write what you want to write. Write your own thing. The best writing comes from experience – so **women write from a woman's point of view** – But I don't think I would commission a script just because it was written by a woman.

There will be more women decision-makers – and it's possible that women writers may find things a little easier. They will be helped by the new independent TV companies such as Hat Trick, Alomo, Talkback, Noel Gay TV and Verity Lambert's TV. Such companies are not dominated by an established tradition of 'men in suits'. Hat Trick, for example, is run by Denise O'Donoghue who has many successful productions to her credit including the award-winning *Drop the Dead Donkey*.

But remember – to be a woman is not enough . . . the script will still have to be good.

A woman who has 'paid her dues' to become one of the decision makers at BBC TV is Rosie Bunting, editor, comedy development.

Rosie Bunting has a most impressive background – in journalism, directing and producing documentaries; she made her name as head of production and development at London Films, then went on to become head of comedy for SelecTV (which includes the companies Alomo, Witzend, and Clement La Frenais).

Maybe it is just a feminine aspect, but I love the team aspect of television production. The skill of the producers is to get all the different skills working together, making something bigger, and better than the sum of the parts.

How did you get from documentaries and drama to comedy like *Birds of a Feather*?

I was asked to look at some scripts which had been submitted ... I did this and made lots of comments. Sometimes I think that women are more conscientious about reading scripts. I read slowly, maybe slower than most people. I think that is because of my experience working in films, and reading film scripts. I believe in reading a script in real time, I like to let it play in front of me.

Marks and Gran liked my comments, and I was asked to join the company. I think I fitted in because Marks and Gran go for a dramatically based comedy.

I love the idea of team writing, I think it is good for new writers to cut their teeth on a show that has already been established.

One thing I've learnt is that some writers will never fit into the team process. You have to cast writers for a team just as carefully as you cast actors to appear in front of camera.

For a lot of English writers it is a very strange thing to sit down round a table and have other writers comment on your work.

Advice to those writers starting out?

It is difficult for new writers to come up with something that's refreshing and different. While there is probably a limit to the settings of a show ... something different can be achieved by making characters with greater complexity. What would be new is someone's point of view of the world ... the way they look at everything.

(An example of this might be *Till Death* and *One Foot in the Grave* – both in domestic settings but made new and different by the characterization of Alf Garnett and Victor Meldrew.)

The other way of achieving something new is what I call the 'tone' of the show. An example of this is M*A*S*H. This could have been just another medical sitcom, but it actually had a dark tone to it.

In order to break in you have initially to do some writing that becomes your calling card. You have to be persistent, watch all the programmes, target the producers, the directors who you think would be interested in your style of writing.

When you are starting out, the more you can see your stuff being performed the better, even if just by some amateur group or your friends.

One way into writing, though a slightly roundabout way, is through performing. Jenny Lecoat wrote a pilot show which has been commissioned for a series by the ITV network, but Jenny Lecoat has been a well-known stand-up comic for many years.

I did loads of Edinburghs, then got established on the cabaret scene – of course I was always writing, but writing my own stand-up material.

My writing experience was building up all the time anyway, I always knew that I didn't want to be a stand-up forever. Partly because I didn't love it enough, and you really have to be emotionally committed to that job to make it work, and also I was slightly too nervous. I never quite lost that last degree of fear that I think you need. I decided I wanted to concentrate on writing – to write comedy for television.

How did you get your first break?

I sent a two-page idea to Alomo, this led to lunch with Rosie Bunting. She didn't like the idea, but she liked some of the phrases in it, and she knew my reputation as a stand-up, so of course that helped.

I came up with another idea, which after many meetings and rewrites became *Sometime Never*, a series commissioned by ITV. I was lucky that I went to an independent company that was willing to spend some time with me and help me develop the idea.

What is the show about? Is it autobiographical?

There are some autobiographical bits in it. There's quite a lot of me in several of the characters. I suppose it is basically about the pursuit of happiness. It is about my own generation of women (I'm thirty-five). The generation that grew up expecting that we were going to have everything: a great career, a fantastic relationship, the great house and the wonderful children. We wanted everything and we wanted it now.

What I think is historically interesting about this generation is that it is the first one ... my mum did not have any of these aspirations because she didn't grow up with the same type of education, or the same type of cultural references.

I think a lot of us have ended up disappointed. You realize you can't have everything. If you are very lucky you can get a lot of one thing, but not everything at once.

In the show there are two main characters, Max and Bernice. Max is thirty-one, she's single, she wanted to be an actress but ended up being a drama teacher, so she feels compromised and she still hasn't found the relationship she is looking for.

In the flat upstairs is her mate Bernice who is quite the opposite. She is married with kids, married young, is deeply unhappy with her marriage, but is kind of stuck with it.

Both of them envy each other's life, but neither would be very happy if they swapped over either. The show is really about wanting what you can't have.

Stand-up gave you certain advantages – did it make you a better writer?

You get very specific and very careful about joke construction and very perfectionist about it. I think the other thing that stand-up gave me in a way is that having been in stand-up for such a long time and hanging around with all the other comics, the dressing-rooms, going on the tours and all that kind of stuff ... I think there is a kind of comedy fitness level you get to that you don't get if you are sitting writing alone.

You need to be out there, you need to develop your sense of humour, but being around people who are funny and by bantering and having funny conversations, that helped a lot – I was mixing with a lot of very funny people. If you spend a lot of time with them then eventually that will start to rub off a bit.

22   The development of alternative comedy

One approach to the question posed in this chapter's title is to look at comedy up to the emergence of what is called 'Alternative'.

Until the 1960s, censorship was fairly rigid in this country. Plays had to be submitted to the Lord Chamberlain's Office for approval, and not just plays but comedy sketches, comedians' routines, in fact anything that was to be performed before an audience.

Anything too sexy, four-letter words, gags about the Royals were just not allowed. Words like 'bloody', even when used by George Bernard Shaw in *Pygmalion*, caused a furore, and as for two men kissing each other in Arthur Miller's *View from the Bridge* – that was out! Banned. It could only be performed in a private theatre club.

These restrictions were naturally the guidelines for TV and radio. Censorship began to ease a little in the 1960s.

There has been much nostalgic talk about the 'Swinging Sixties', but there was very little swinging at the BBC. Auntie kept her beady eyes on us all.

In the 1960s, Ronald Chesney and I were writing *The Rag Trade*. In our script there was a scene in a pub with Barbara Windsor. A chap who rather fancied her was trying to get her drunk. He kept plying her with cocktails. When he wasn't looking she was pouring most of the booze into a goldfish bowl on the pub counter. Auntie Beeb thought this was shocking! We were accused of being cruel to goldfish, and that bit of the script was cut.

Another example was in *Steptoe and Son*. The writers, Galton and Simpson, had the father and son shouting 'Cobblers' at each other. The Beeb didn't like that . . .

142

'Cobblers' was not a BBC word. After some argument it was agreed that 'cobblers' could be used – but on the strict understanding that it was used only twice in each script. This solved the problem for a while. Then one week Galton and Simpson went to the controller to say: 'In this week's episode we have only used 'cobblers' once. Can we carry one lot of 'cobblers' forward to next week?'

There were plenty of shock waves when Alf Garnett came on the scene. The controllers didn't like Alf referring to his wife as 'Silly Cow'. This was felt to be far too strong and was watered down to 'Silly Moo'. I think the only four-letter expletive officially approved by the Beeb in those days was 'Gosh'!

Sitcoms developed in this atmosphere had self-imposed restrictions. Nothing very nasty or unpleasant ever really happened. In the traditional sitcom, whatever the problem or predicament, it would somehow be resolved and everybody would be more or less back to normal at the end of the episode.

If the show opened with the star suffering from terrible pains in the chest, it would eventually turn out to be something like indigestion, and not a fatal heart attack.

If the show opened with someone winning a fortune on the pools, we all knew that something would have to go wrong – the football coupon had not been posted – there had been some kind of mistake. No-one was going to end up stinking rich, because that would completely alter the format.

If the show opened with the husband suspecting his wife of being unfaithful, and acting in a most suspicious way, eventually there would be a perfectly acceptable innocent explanation.

In the traditional sitcom of that day, people did not die, did not get filthy rich, and did not sleep around.

Although censorship has all but disappeared, some sitcoms still cling to the traditional guidelines, while in others such as *Men Behaving Badly, Drop the Dead Donkey*, and even *One Foot in the Grave*, people do die and do sleep around. But even the most modern sitcom is not labelled 'alternative'. This label is given to stand-up comics.

Let us look then at those billed or described as 'alternative'. Who are they? They are usually quite young and often found their way into show business via university revue and at venues like the Edinburgh Festival.

What is different about their material? Most of them use the four-letter words with great frequency.

Older stand-up comics such as the late Frankie Howerd and Les Dawson never used these words in their act. Maybe coarser language is more acceptable from the younger and better educated. Frankie Howerd once quipped: 'You can't say "fuck" on television unless you've been to university.'

The most refreshing thing about these new comics is that their material and their targets for humour are different. They don't usually gag about wives and mother-in-law, and the hackneyed subjects. Their material is often more intelligent. Some of them are angry and make social comments about the police, discrimination, living on the front line in Brixton – subjects that the older comics would not dare to tackle.

Warren Mitchell is a great admirer of alternative comedy:

> The question always asked is, what is alternative? And alternative to what? In my mind, alternative comedy is honest . . . Comedy has always been dirty . . . smutty . . . Alternative comedy does not use euphemisms . . . does not have lines like, 'I am going home to stroke my pussy'.
>
> They talk about sex – not 'it'. Alternative comics say what they mean, and are not frightened of tackling any subject.
>
> In his last series, Ben Elton did a mime routine about a girl trying to fit in a diaphragm which kept springing out.
>
> This having fun, and also making a comment on a problem that girls go through – a very real problem – was not dirty or smutty, it was honest.

Tony Robinson, on alternative comedy:

> I don't think the categories 'alternative' and 'mainstream' are particularly helpful.
>
> It might be better to say that there is accurate comedy and lazy comedy. I think what a number of young comics in the eighties tried to do was to find new contemporary targets for their jokes . . . to get away from the stock butts of comedy . . . the mother-in-law . . . the wife . . . the golf-course.

As times became more permissive there were new targets for their humour.

Alternative comics claim to have swept away all barriers, but there is one other factor:

In the campaign against Aids, there are even programmes instructing teenagers how to use a condom by putting one on to a banana and rolling it down. Once viewers have seen that, I don't think they can be surprised by anything. It is arguable that Aids has done more than anything to do away with any form of censorship. Even the most middle-of-the-road comedies now have the almost obligatory jokes about condoms. What was once banned as bad taste is now positively encouraged, to prevent the disease.

23   Drama and comedy –
The same tricks

Comedy writers are not that different from drama writers or straight writers. They are not from another planet . . . they don't eat special food.

We all use the same tricks. The writer's friend – what goes wrong? – is used just as much in drama as in comedy.

We have all seen the James Bond films which open with James Bond handcuffed, tied up and about to be killed, and the villain saying, 'Before I kill you, Mr Bond, I can't resist showing you my special plans for conquering the world.' He unties Bond, but of course something goes wrong. Bond escapes and we are off on a two-hour adventure.

In nearly every murder mystery, carefully planned robberies, something goes wrong to heighten the tension, just as in comedy it goes wrong to give the laughs.

INFIDELITY
Having an affair and something goes wrong – the lovers are found out.

This is often used in farce and comedy, but it is also used with great effect by Harold Pinter in his play *Betrayal*.

A wife is having an affair with her husband's best friend. The wife is on holiday with her husband in Venice.

What goes wrong? A letter from her lover is given to her husband by mistake.

From then on the inter-play between the characters leads to some brilliant writing by Pinter.

A GROUP OF DISPARATE CHARACTERS FORCED TOGETHER BY
CIRCUMSTANCE

This situation always produces the conflict that both drama
and comedy writers are looking for.

Take a group of prisoners being given a hard time by some
of the warders.

Written one way, this situation could be a comedy show
like *Porridge*. Written another way by a straight writer, it
could be a high drama about prison life, as in films like *San
Quentin* and *Alcatraz*.

UNIFORMS

Straight writers, just like comedy writers, use uniforms to
give immediate information to the audience. Think of all the
police films, the army films, the hospital films and series, and
of course all those cowboys and Indians. When the Apaches
were attacking the waggon train you didn't need a single plot
line to tell who was who.

THE CHARACTERS IN COMEDY AND GOOD DETECTIVE SERIES.

Comedy writers know the advantage of creating strong
characters. Writers of detective series – inspired by Sherlock
Holmes and Poirot – try every trick to build a character.
There's Ironside in the wheelchair, Kojak the bald-headed
detective who's always sucking a lollipop, Columbo with
squint and limp and dirty raincoat.

THE STORY LINE:

A film like *The Guns of Navarone* is well worth studying for
would-be comedy writers. It has all the basic tricks that we
used.

The film opens during World War Two, at an RAF base in
Italy. (Note: Everyone's in uniform. We know we're in Italy –
there is a map on the wall – VISUAL INFORMATION.)

A bomber squadron has just come back from a raid, badly
mauled . . . they've lost yet more planes trying to bomb those
powerful long-distance guns at Navarone which are
destroying British convoys. The commander says, 'We can't
win the war unless those guns are destroyed.' (Note: That's
the plot.)

This well-written screenplay by Carl Foreman sets up the

plot in the first two or three minutes. There are no more plot lines – just a series of adventures and twists until the guns are finally destroyed.

This film became a classic. The story line, though simple, was strong. No plot scenes, much adventure. Which is what the comedy writer tries to achieve – the minimum of plotting, and plenty of laughs.

When you study comedy and drama writing, you will find that there is very little basic difference. Mostly it is a matter of treatment. It is a difference of style, not of substance.

Marks and Gran – who have always believed in stretching their talents – ventured into drama writing. This experience resulted in the successful *Goodnight Sweetheart*, which will undoubtedly be a cult show of the future.

Goodnight Sweetheart is a time-warp comedy starring Nicholas Lyndhurst who finds he can wander from the present day back into the 1940s and wartime England.

This show is original, different, an immediate success. But how did it happen? Where did the idea come from?

Micheál Jacob – script executive for *Goodnight Sweetheart*:

> The show began as an idea for a stage play, set in present and wartime London. Marks and Gran have always been fascinated by World War Two, and as they played with the idea it became more clearly a television project and was seen as a potential vehicle for Nicholas Lyndhurst.

Over the years Marks and Gran have had a string of sitcom successes, the early ones being quite traditional such as *Holding the Fort*, a role reversal with the wife as an army officer while her husband stayed at home to mind the baby, and *Relative Strangers*, a single parent idea about a happy-go-lucky father who finds he has an unexpected teenage son to cope with.

They went on to break new ground with *Birds of a Feather*.

> But Marks and Gran have never seen themselves entirely as sitcom writers. They had written *Harvey Moon*, a fifty-minute comedy drama, *Love Hurts*, and the full length drama *Wall of Silence*. I don't think they could have written *Sweetheart* if they hadn't written drama as well.

24   *Corporate videos*

Comedy writers should be eternally grateful to John Cleese. In the 1960s, Cleese made some staff training videos which were different. They were wildly successful, and successful because they were funny.

Cleese paved the way. It is now accepted that the humorous approach can be effective in getting the message across, and comedy writers are often called in to script a corporate or educational video.

How does a writer go about this type of work?

Let's look at a teaching aid video I wrote for ILEA, the now defunct Inner London Education Authority.

The subject was Land Law – the legal problems in house purchase. In a twenty-minute video you can get across about a dozen points – no more.

These points had to be decided on in conjunction with a working party of lawyers and teachers.

Land Law is a hefty subject, and doesn't easily lend itself to humour. Here are a couple of examples of the points that had to be made in house purchase.

The first example is to show the difference between the survey made for a building society, and the survey for the purchaser.

THE SCENE IS THE FRONT DOOR OF A SUBURBAN HOUSE.

A MIDDLE-AGED COUPLE ARE AT THE DOOR.
A POSTMAN IS HANDING OVER A BULKY REGISTERED PACKAGE.

HUSBAND: Look. The deeds from the building society. The
           mortgage is finished. No more payments.

WIFE: Isn't it marvellous? After twenty-five years the
             house is ours. All ours.

             THEY GO INSIDE, SLAMMING THE FRONT DOOR.
             THERE IS A SHOWER OF TILES FROM THE ROOF,
             FOLLOWED BY BRICKS FALLING. THEN, WITH THE
             AID OF SPECIAL EFFECTS, THE HOUSE SLOWLY
             COLLAPSES.

During this, a voice-over explained that the building
society survey was only concerned that the house remained
standing as security for the period of the loan.

From the cold-blooded legal point of view, the building
society is not really concerned if the house falls down when
the last payment is made, after twenty-five years. The
house-buyer, of course, is.

The business of the house collapsing, which was of course
done with special effects, was a bit crazy. But the student is
more likely to remember a point if it is associated with a
much larger-than-life exaggerated picture.

Another point to be made in house-purchase was the
importance of checking any planning applications or
proposed developments.

    THE SCENE WAS THE SUNNY BACK GARDEN OF A 'JUST SOLD'
    HOUSE.
    A YOUNG COUPLE WERE SUNNING THEMSELVES IN THE QUIET,
    SECLUDED GARDEN.
    THEN, WITH SPECIAL EFFECTS, THERE WAS SUPERIMPOSED A
    HIGH-RISE BLOCK OF FLATS NEXT DOOR, TOWERING OVER THE
    GARDEN AND BLOCKING OUT THE SUN.
    A FACTORY WAS ON THE OTHER SIDE.
    A MOTORWAY ACROSS THE BACK.
    AND A LOW-FLYING AIRCRAFT WAS SCREAMING OVER THEM.

Again, a crazy, wildly exaggerated picture, but it helped
the student to remember to check all possible developments
that might be in the pipeline from property development, new
roads, and even airport runway extensions.

The style of writing depends greatly on the subject matter.

Sometimes a corporate video has to deal with a sensitive
issue.

I worked on one for the Manpower Services Commission. The video was aimed at the long-term unemployed to persuade them to brush up their job-interview technique.

Now there is nothing funny about being unemployed for a long time, and it can be somewhat insulting telling a person how to dress and behave at an interview.

A gentle approach was decided upon.

Preparing and going to a job interview was compared with going on a blind date. Dressing carefully to project the right image, and finding out as much as you could about the job offer – just as you might try and find out as much as possible about the date.

All the necessary points were made by comparison and example – instead of saying 'Do this or Do that' and appearing to talk down to and lecturing the unemployed.

This idea was low-key and amusing, and apparently quite successful when shown at job-centres.

The big problem that the comedy writer has when first doing corporate work is that you are not hired to write what you want to write; you are hired to get across certain information and certain facts; not to go off on some tangent of your own, no matter how funny.

You have to please the clients. They are paying you. They buy outright. They can do what they like with your script. Alter it; rewrite. They have bought it. It's theirs, and, of course, there are no residuals or repeat fees.

The advantages are that a video script is usually about twenty minutes long, and only takes between a week and ten days to write. It is not a long-term involvement and can be fitted in between other jobs, to keep you ticking over.

25 Working abroad

Should I go to Hollywood?

To be a success in Hollywood you don't have to travel far. In fact, you need go no further west than the BBC Television Centre, White City, London, Thames Television at Teddington, Granada, Yorkshire, Central, or any one of the independent television companies throughout Britain who sell to the States.

The best way to make it in the States is to achieve some measure of success over here.

If you can't make it in your home town, then I would say it is almost impossible for a Brit, unknown and with no track record, to make it over there. Nowadays the output from British television is closely monitored by the Americans. The networks, the independents, the distributors, either have offices over here or have arrangements with agents here who send them details of every new comedy show.

Brian Cooke and Johnny Mortimer were working for Thames TV when American interest in British comedy was starting to grow.

Brian Cooke:

> Johnny and I were writing *Man About the House*, which was doing quite well, with Richard O'Sullivan and Paula Wilcox. It was very popular.
>
> An American TV distributor – Don Taffner – saw its possibilities and the show was adapted for the American audience, that is, the entire show was remade in the States with American actors, and with our scripts adapted by American writers. It was given a new title – *Three's Company*.

Don Taffner masterminded the operation – his expertise and knowledge of the American market helped make the show a fantastic success, also a financial success – my share of the royalties have made me financially self-sufficient.

The success of *Man About the House* certainly put Brian Cooke into the millionaire class, and also helped launch many 'spin-offs' and set up new shows for the American networks.

This all sounds very easy – a nice smooth ride to megabucks, but it doesn't always happen that way.

THIS IS THE PROCEDURE:

The option

An American company wants to buy an option on your show. Not megabucks yet, usually between five and ten thousand dollars.

They will try and get the option for a period of five years.

You argue that five years is too long, you try and get it down to six months or one year, but if you're a writer without a track record you may have to settle for two years. At the end of that time, if they can't sell the show, all the rights revert to you. And all you've got is a few thousand pounds.

The pilot script

Having got the option, the company's next move is to have a pilot script written, but they'll only do this if they sound out a few people and feel there might be some interest in the project.

The pilot script is probably one of your scripts rewritten by American writers.

Sometimes you may be asked to go to Los Angeles for a few weeks to collaborate. All expenses are paid, and your fee might be something like fifty thousand dollars.

Making the pilot show

Unfortunately, this may never happen. To make a pilot show can cost upwards of a million dollars. Not every pilot script is made into a show. Hundreds of pilot scripts are commissioned every year, possibly five hundred, but only about fifty of these are chosen to be made.

But let's assume your script is actually made into a pilot – we press on to the next stage:

Selling the pilot

The pilot is shown to programme controllers. Out of the fifty odd pilots being shown around, maybe about a dozen are taken up by the networks and a series of six or thirteen commissioned.

On air – The new season

The dozen surviving shows are transmitted in the new season, which is mid- to late September.

The ratings

If a new show does not get a good rating in the first weeks it is dropped, usually cut off after the sixth episode. If a dozen new shows are launched, usually only two or three survive. They may go for one season and carry on for two or three or anything up to five years. Then all concerned, including the writers, are wallowing in megabucks. But the odds are at least a thousand to one. Competition between the rival networks is fierce. Every point in the ratings represents millions of dollars in advertising revenue. Schedules are altered as networks attack each other ruthlessly. As one TV executive said to me: 'It's war! And we don't take prisoners.'

ADVENTURES IN TINSELTOWN

The stories of the adventures of British writers in the States are weird and wonderful.

Somehow, several British shows have survived the system and go on the air, but it's never been easy.

There were several attempts to adapt *Steptoe and Son* for the States. The trouble was that the English rag and bone men did not exist over there. One pilot was made with an Italian and his son running a fruit and vegetable stall. Eventually they cast a black nightclub comedian, Red Foxx, as the father, found an excellent young black actor for the son, Desmond Wilson, and the show worked.

In the States, *Steptoe and Son* has been retitled *Sanford and Son*, and has been a great success. Many episodes of

Sanford and Son have used the original English script, with very little change.

Another British show that was changed out of all recognition was *Till Death Us Do Part*. Alf Garnett became Archie Bunker. Though very little of the original scripts were used, the show – which was now called *All in the Family* – held the top slot in the American ratings for five years.

Porridge – starring Ronnie Barker, and beautifully written by Dick Clement and Ian la Frenais – was a show that the Americans bought but really didn't know what to do with. The problem was the casting. Ronnie Barker played the unsuccessful small-time burglar — not a violent man, but one who was warm-hearted and lovable in spite of his criminal tendencies.

But there didn't seem to be an equivalent Ronnie Barker in the States and, besides, they don't really have lovable burglars (neither do we any more).

In the event, *Porridge* became *On the Rocks* in the States. The characters were much harder and, at times, quite violent.

The show, which might have been a hit if it had been handled differently, did not meet with much success.

After the success of *On the Buses*, the Americans decided to buy the show, and I think the experiences that Chesney and I had were typical.

To borrow a phrase from another writer: 'It was the best of times, it was the worst of times.'

Americans like to buy success, then wonder why they bought it. NBC bought *On the Buses* because it was consistently top of the ratings and won award after award. The fact that a show about a cockney bus driver was hardly suitable for adaptation for the States was considered of minor importance.

In the event, the show was set in the lost and found department of a Greyhound bus depot, and no bus was seen in any of the twenty-six American episodes.

Knowing some of the pitfalls from other British writers, we were a bit wary. We wanted assurances about the director and the American writers.

We were thrilled to be told that the director would be Carl Reiner. What they didn't tell us was that Carl Reiner was to direct the pilot show only.

We were delighted to know that the scripts would be rewritten by the writers of the *Dick van Dyke Show*, Bill Persky and Sam Denoff, a well-known and highly regarded team.

We worked together, but there was a bit of a problem with the language. When we got together with the cast at NBC studios in Burbank for a 'read thru', one of the first lines in our script was: 'Olive, where's the torch? I can't find the spanner.' None of the American cast knew what that meant until it was translated into: 'Olive, where's the flashlight? I can't find the monkey wrench.'

But these were just minor problems. So far, everything had gone remarkably well.

There had been no problems. Everything went very smoothly – almost too smoothly – as regards setting up that show. There was the option, the pilot script, the making of the pilot, the programme controller loved the plot and ordered thirteen episodes with an option of another thirteen.

The show was retitled *Lotsa Luck* and starred Dom Delouise. It opened to good reviews in Los Angeles and New York, though not quite so good in the Mid-West. Nevertheless, it built quite nicely and was in a comfortable position in the ratings.

Our agent told us that options were being picked up and a five-year contract was being negotiated for our services.

Then disaster struck! Somebody at the network decided to reschedule our show, and put it in another slot. The guy figured that our show was doing so well that he could put it up against the *American Football World Series* on the opposite channel. This is the equivalent in England to having your show put up against the Cup Final – each week!

Our show, of course, plummeted in the ratings. Options were not taken up, and the show was dropped for the next season.

We went back to Hollywood to try and sell another show. This time it was very, very different. To be in Hollywood when your show has been dropped, with no contract, makes you a non-person. People who we thought were friends kept away from us as if we had the plague. They seemed to regard success and failure like an infection. Mix with success, and you become successful! Mix with failure, and you flop.

It was also difficult to talk to anybody at the studio where we had worked for months and – even worse – almost impossible to get through to our agent. The reply from his secretary was: 'Sorry, he's at a meeting. We'll call you back.'

But this was the American system. When they want you, you are cosseted, pampered and given the best of everything. We had the best rooms in the best hotels, a daily allowance, and were extremely well paid. When the contract finished, everything else finished – abruptly.

But that's the system – that's the way it is. If you don't like it, well, nobody forces you to go.

When devising a show for British TV, should it be slanted to appeal to the Americans?

This has been tried many times. It just hasn't worked out. You end up trying to please too many people by writing what we call a Mid-Atlantic show. And there is a saying in the business that Mid-Atlantic shows are for weather-ships.

What type of British show succeeds in the States?

It is hard to generalize, but the only clue I can offer is this:

Shows that rely on relationships seem to travel better than shows with a strong background.

For example: *Man About the House* – two girls sharing a flat with a boy is a relationship, it doesn't have to be in any particular country.

Dear John – by John Sullivan – is successful in the States. It is about a group of divorced people. Again, this set-up could happen – in fact does happen – anywhere in the Western world.

Steptoe also works – again, a relationship between father and son.

It does seem that strong relationships adapt better than a show with a strong background. But, as always, there are no rules.

OTHER MARKETS

The Dutch, the Scandinavians and the Germans have a high regard for British comedy and British comedy writers, and buy a lot of English scripts.

How do you contact them?

Again, you don't have to. All the important producers and networks have their associates in England. These associates know what their producers are looking for. They know the market. They have a fair idea of what might be acceptable in Bavaria, Holland, or Sweden.

They watch every show, and if they think that your show might be suitable they will approach you or your agent.

The deal is pretty straightforward. The Dutch, the Germans, or the Swedes will buy your scripts – they usually want all the rights, but for their territory only. For this you get a lump sum. This may be for what we call a complete buy-out, that is, no repeat fees or royalties. Or for a lesser sum they have the right to transmit the show once only, and then a repeat fee for every transmission.

The producers then have the script translated into their own language, and completely remade using their own actors.

Nearly all the top British shows have been sold and remade this way. There have been Swedish language versions of *Hancock's Half Hour* and *The Rag Trade*, Dutch versions of *Steptoe and Son, On the Buses, Till Death Us Do Part*, and many others.

The advantage to these buyers is that they can acquire a batch of 13, 26 or 39 episodes, all written, tried and trusted. They are not particularly concerned if the show is a few years old. In 1989, the Swedes bought *The Rag Trade*, which was last shown in England in 1978. The pile of scripts which many writers have on their shelves can become nice little earners.

Original scripts are also commissioned

The Dutch and the Germans will often ask British writers to devise a show for one of their own performers. You don't have to write in Dutch or German, you write in English.

The procedure is quite simple – this is how it went for us:

Chesney and I were contacted by Andrew Mann – an English literary agent who was the UK representative for a leading Dutch producer.

The producer wanted a show starring Andre Van Duin, a Dutch entertainer – something in the style of Benny Hill.

We were flown to Amsterdam for the weekend to meet the star and the producer and discuss the layout of the show, then we settled down to a regular working pattern.

We spent the week writing, then every Saturday we'd fly to Amsterdam for a script readthrough – our script being translated on the spot by one of the Dutch production team who was completely bilingual.

As a general rule, working for the Dutch, the Swedes or the Germans is more relaxing than working for the Americans. You don't get the pressure, the hassle, or the tension. But although it is well paid, you don't get the megabucks.

Unfortunately, it seems that the tension and pressure increases in direct proportion to the amount of money that can be earnt.

All this may seem lovely and exciting, but honestly, it is most unlikely to happen unless you achieve some success over here first.

Changed formats

Beryl Vertue pioneered the 'changed format' deal. She managed to sell to the Americans the format and scripts of *Steptoe and Sons* and even *Till Death Do Us Part*, which was considered almost impossible at the time.

> They were very nervous about *Till Death*. They were worried about the controversy and the bigotry. They were scared. But the show under it's American name of *All In The Family*, has become one of the most successful shows ever on American TV.

Men Behaving Badly has now been bought by Carsey Werner, the US independent TV company which makes *Roseanne* and *The Bill Cosby Show*.

> I have learnt from my previous experience. Who is doing it? That's what I want to know. Not which network, not which building, but who is doing it? Who are the writers? Will they understand what makes the show work? If you are not going to be controversial. If the men are not going to behave badly, then I have to say, don't do it, don't buy it, there's nothing to buy.

26   *Breaking in*

It has been said that selling your work is part of the talent of being a writer.

There's a lot in that saying. The brain that thinks up ideas should think out a way of selling them.

Who is going to buy scripts or give me a break?
TV and radio producers and directors.

Which ones?
Study the shows. Is there a producer or director who uses the sort of sketch material or scripts that you write?

Sketch shows will often buy an unsolicited sketch. If it goes well, the producer will look favourably on your next submissions and might eventually commission material.

If you want to be a sitcom writer, you have to submit a script.

There are two schools of thought about this. You can write a sample episode of a successful sitcom which is already running. The producer can then compare your work directly with the work of established writers. If it compares well, the producer might be impressed and be able to put some work your way.

But other producers are not particularly interested in your version of an established show. They want to see something that's new and different – something which shows that the writer has an original talent.

WAYS TO GET NOTICED BY PRODUCERS AND DIRECTORS
People in the business are always impressed if you have a play running almost anywhere. It is unlikely to be in the West End,

but it is sometimes possible to get a comedy put on at one of the smaller theatres, or maybe the Fringe.

One of our finest and most prolific comedy writers, Eric Chappell, got his break when a play of his had a short run at the Hampstead Theatre. This led directly to his series *Rising Damp* with Leonard Rossiter, Richard Beckinsale and Frances de la Tour. From then on, there was no looking back.

Radio is still reckoned by some to be the best way into writing.

Andy Hamilton:

> When I started the most important years were the first two years along the corridors of Light Entertainment Radio. There were a lot of very good people there like Griff Rhys Jones, John Lloyd and Geoff Perkins. (NB Lloyd became producer of *Spitting Image*. Perkins helped form Hat Trick Productions and was, for many years, head of comedy at BBC TV.)
>
> We did loads of shows, some probably not that good, some very original. The main thing was that we were in and out of each other's offices. We used to play football in the corridor. We were young writers and producers . . . we sort of sparked off each other. We became friends and used to work in various combinations. We got used to being quite trusting with each other. Those early years were great fun. There was a sense of controlled anarchy about the place.
>
> There is no golden rule for breaking in. Doing radio is a sensible way to build your skill base. Even the most experienced and successful writers get their stuff rejected. Rejection is part of the game. This is one of the areas where the writer's experience is close to the actor's. You have to learn to develop a thick skin. When you are starting out don't be afraid to take on anything that comes along. As long as you keep an idea in your own mind of the thing that you ultimately want to do. Young writers should be pretty catholic and not be too snooty about what they do.

Micheál Jacob is in charge of script development for situation comedies and half-hour comedy dramas at BBC Television.

Is team-writing a way to break in? Do you think team-writing is the way forward?

> That depends on the type of show. *My Family* started as a team show and runs like an American team. This probably

wouldn't work on a show like *My Hero* or *The Office*.

One of the problems with team-writing is that young writers don't want to write mainstream, but aspire to a more whacky type of show. However, if a writer comes to the BBC with a good idea, and we think it will run, the writer must be prepared for other people to write it.

The first series is usually for six or seven episodes. If it goes well, and a further series of fourteen or fifteen episodes is planned, then other writers must be used.

A new writer doesn't have to submit a whole series, but one complete script and a good idea of where the show might go.

In the States, in an average year, about 300 scripts are commissioned, and from these about forty pilots are made. From these forty pilots, maybe six might get on the air, and only one might survive. No one has found a perfect way of testing shows; until the show goes out, you never know.

What's the procedure? What happens when a script arrives on your desk?

If I like it, I meet the writer. If it is a brand new writer, then they must send in a complete script. There is no other way.

I work on the script with the writer, and give notes for a rewrite. If I like the rewrite, I take the script to head of department Sophie Clark-Gervais, and if she likes it, she may commission a second script. If that goes well, a producer is attached to the project and it then goes to the channel controller. If the controller likes it, a read-through is organized with the cast we want. Sometimes a new actor gets a chance, but usually the people who commission shows always feel happier with a face they know.

Whatever happens at the read-through, we would not go into production unless we had six scripts we were happy with.

Are you bombarded with scripts?

We get about 2,500 a year, but I'm afraid only a few of them show real talent. I try to read about six scripts a day, and I think from the first few pages I know whether they are any good. If I don't laugh by page five, I panic and dip into the script a bit later. Most certainly I would know the value of a script by page ten.

At the BBC we are always looking for comedy writing talent, and I am convinced that this talent will always be recognized.

Ian Brown:

Team-writing as such – that is, a show that was intended to be written by a team from its very beginning – never really existed in the UK. Shows like *Drop the Dead Donkey*, *Birds of a Feather*, *Goodnight Sweetheart* and *'Allo 'Allo* would be written by its originators and creators for several series. Then other writers might be brought in to help out. That was as far as team-writing went. These other writers were almost always very experienced with good track records.

My Family was the first show in the UK to be team-written in the American style; that is, written by a team from the very outset.

How did My Family *start?*

The idea was thought up by Fred Barron, who pitched it to the BBC. Fred had created and written for many shows in the States, including *Seinfeld* and *Frasier*. Fred is the executive producer, or what is known in the States as the 'show runner'. Apart from Fred, there were two other American writers, brothers Jim and Steve Armogida, and two Brits, James Hendric and me [Ian Brown]. Fred's aim was to create a stable of British writers who would get used to working the American way.

What is the American way?

All the writers work out the plots as a team. They then split up to write the first draft of the actual episodes. The first draft may take about ten days. The show is recorded at Pinewood Studios, and the hours of rewriting take place in the writers' room where the whole team go through the first draft script, line by line.

When the show is in production, the writers are paid a daily rate to be there every day. If any rewrites are required, the writers are there on hand.

What is the weekly routine?

On Friday morning we have our first read-through.

Are all the writers there?

Yes, and we would all be fairly happy with the script; we would all have been through it round the table in the writers' room. As *My Family* is made by an independent company, someone from the BBC would also be at the read-through.

We then go back to the writers' room to deal with any notes from the BBC, and then go back to the cast for a second read-through. At this second read-through anybody in the cast can pipe up and say 'I don't understand this line' or 'could I have a better joke?', and sometimes if there is a scene the cast are not happy with, we go back to the writers' room and start rewriting. We usually finish this about 7 p.m., though one week we didn't finish until three in the morning. We have Saturday and Sunday off. On Monday we work on the following week's script to get it up to standard for the following Friday morning.

We record on Thursday. Thursday is show day. Then on the next day – Friday morning, it all starts again.

[But a word of warning from Ian Brown.] Not all writers are suitable to be part of a team. Before you go into the writers' room, you must leave your ego outside the door!

This first attempt at American style team-writing has been a great success.

Alan Plater:

Do you have any tips for young writers?

Write lots and, when you're not writing, read lots. A good public library is your academy and it's free. When I was starting I read every radio and television play that was in print. I can still quote scenes from some of them – plus dozens of stage plays, old and new. I also read books by and about writers; David Mamet's essays, Arthur Miller's autobiography, Raymond Chandler's letters and notebooks are among my favourites. This homework goes on forever.

All good writers are nosy parkers who want to know everything about everything. You should want to know everything about people: how they talk; how they think; how they move about; and the wonderful poetry of everyday speech whereby every single person in the human race sounds different.

Every good writer has a good ear for what is unique and extraordinary about people. Nobody is ordinary. The poetry may be hidden, but it's there. Our job is to find it and give it voice. Listen to the music and work out words.

Men Behaving Badly started life as a book which came to the notice of Beryl Vertue – a leading independent producer.

There was something about the book, the blurb, and the title that attracted me. I quite liked the title.

It was written by a young man called Simon Nye. He had written this book, but he hadn't done anything else. I asked him to adapt the book for situation comedy. He hadn't written for television before, but he is a very quick learner.

He had what I think is so important for comedy: really good characters, and he wrote very funny dialogue – quirky.

I took it to Thames TV, and after two series it won the award for Best ITV Comedy of the year.

This was a fantastic achievement for a new writer like Simon Nye, but he was soon to learn that things do not go that smoothly in this business. The show was dropped by ITV because it did not have a high enough viewing.

But Beryl Vertue had great faith in the show.

I thought the show had more potential; I managed to persuade the BBC to take it on. It was risky, but they decided to schedule the show to go out at a later time. This way you could be a bit ruder, and behave a bit more badly. This paid off, and the show has gone from success to success. This is not just beginner's luck for Simon Nye. His new show *Is It Legal?*, after its first series, won the British Comedy Award for 1995. Simon was a translator in a bank before writing sitcoms. He was that rarity who just found he could do it.

Jack Rosenthal:

My first job with Granada TV was writing promotion material.

So when Tony Warren started *Coronation Street* I had an intro. Initially I started work on *Coronation Street* for thirteen episodes, but ended up writing two hundred episodes altogether. I found the discipline invaluable when I went on to write situation comedy, TV plays and films.

Working on a soap opera seems to have given Rosenthal a wide range. He went on to write a sitcom, *The Dustbin Men*, and a gentle comedy classic *The Lovers* starring Richard Beckinsale and Paula Wilcox; award-winning TV plays such as *Barmitzvah Boy* and *The Knowledge*, and even made it to Hollywood to write the feature film *Yentl* for Barbra Streisand. What is particularly interesting is Rosenthal's range. More recently he wrote the film *London's Burning*, which led to a most successful series produced by London Weekend.

Rosenthal's first break came because he'd taken a job writing promotion material – that is, writing the continuity announcements about forthcoming programmes. But he was in the Granada TV studios and met producers.

Does it help to know producers and directors?

Of course it does. This is where actors who start writing have an advantage.

Jonathan Lynn started writing some scripts with George Layton for *Doctor in the House* when they were both regular actors in the series. London Weekend Television also produced *On the Buses*, and when some extra episodes were needed, Lynn and Layton were asked to write some of the scripts.

Jonathan Lynn then teamed up with Antony Jay to write *Yes Minister*. More recently he wrote and directed *Nuns on the Run* which was well received in the States, and right now he is a Hollywood writer and director. His films include *My Cousin Vinny* and the remake of *Sergeant Bilko*.

There's no doubt an advantage in actually working in the studio, but we can't all be scene-shifters, promotion writers or actors.

Send samples of your work to anyone in the business who might conceivably offer you work. Then don't just sit back and wait, keep up the attack. I don't mean make yourself a nuisance, but at intervals send out – if you've got it – some new material.

If a producer sees first one, then two, then maybe three promising ideas, he is almost bound to get in touch with you.

STUDY THE TRADE PAPERS

Not just the *TV Times* and the *Radio Times*, but *Broadcast Magazine*, *The Stage* and *Screen International*.

Look for clues about who might be wanting what. See if you can spot an opening.

Keep a weather eye on that small group of bankable TV names, like Penelope Keith, Richard Briers, Nigel Havers, Michael Elphick, David Jason. Is the show that they are in now running out of steam and coming to an end? Maybe in the near future the networks will be looking for a new vehicle for one of their favourites.

Much casting is done from people who are already appearing on TV. Is there any up-and-coming actor in a supporting role whom the networks might be interested in grooming? Do you have an idea which would be of use?

David Jason proved himself in supporting roles, and then he was suggested for *Only Fools and Horses*.

Nicholas Lyndhurst made a success of his supporting role in *Only Fools and Horses*, and then starred in his own shows – *The Two of Us* and *Goodnight Sweetheart*.

One of the hit shows of the 1970s was *The Good Life*. It starred Richard Briers and Felicity Kendall. The supporting actors were the relatively unknown Paul Eddington and Penelope Keith who went on to become stars in their own right. Penelope Keith in *To the Manor Born*, and Paul Eddington in *Yes Minister*.

It's so often like that – one TV show begets another. Keep an eye open for the up-and-coming talent.

Can that spark they showed in a small role be developed in the way that Penelope Keith's snobbish neighbour in *The Good Life* developed into the lady of the manor in *To the Manor Born*?

'There will always be a shortage of comedy writers', says Robin Nash – BBC's former head of comedy and executive producer/director of *Bread* and director of *Goodnight Sweetheart*.

> There are of course many writers, but they can't write comedy because very few have this God-given talent. If you have the ability, then the opportunities are there: everyone is looking for comedy.
>
> Generally speaking, new young writers start writing first some form of broken comedy. I mean gags ... quickies ... sketches ... and then graduate to learning the structure of situation comedy. Most of our successful sitcom writers didn't emerge until their mature years, and I think you've got to have that experience – that way of looking at life that only comes with maturity.
>
> I always say to writers, 'go away and write what you know about because that is what you will write best'. I think that for

about eighty per cent of the time this probably works. Roy Clarke writes about the North . . . John Sullivan writes about London, and Carla Lane writes about Liverpool.

Controllers and producers must have confidence in their writers

The first episode of *Dad's Army* was shown to three different audiences, all of whom gave it the thumbs down. The controllers had to go ahead on their own hunches.

What other openings are there for a comedy writer?

Try everything, the Edinburgh Festival, the fringe, even the stand-up at the local pub, summer shows, pantomime, as long as what you write is to the best of your ability in the circumstances, and good of its kind.

Would an agent help me?

It is unlikely that an agent would be interested in a writer with absolutely no track record.

If, however, you have somehow managed to get a small measure of success, then an agent can exploit it, build on it, put you up for new projects, and give you information that you are most unlikely to get yourself; an agent can arrange introductions and guide and groom you through your career.

So, once again, it boils down to you to break in somehow. It is tough – but certainly not impossible. Keep reminding yourself that there is a big demand for good, original comedy writing.

If you have real talent, it will be recognized – but you must be persistent. No one is going to come knocking on your door.

You must keep on trying – that way and this way; this way and that way.

Keep Dodging and Diving, Trying and Striving, and GOOD LUCK!

27 Let's get technical

The writer doesn't really have to know too much about the technical side of things. Think of it as driving a car: You can be a very good driver ... you know what a car can do, but you don't have to know the theory of the internal combustion engine or the differential gearbox.

Nevertheless, it is useful to have a grasp of the basics, and know some of the technical terms in common use when writing for radio, television and films.

Radio
Here is a short sketch or quickie:

	GRANNIE'S FUNERAL
FX:	PHONE RINGS. RECEIVER OFF HOOK
ROGER:	Hello . . . Roger Wilcox here.
BASIL:	(SLIGHT DISTORT) Roger . . . (EXCITED) Roger! How are you, old son? Great news! I've got two tickets for Wembley. Can you get away from the office?
ROGER:	(NERVOUSLY) Oh, no. Not this week, the Boss would never let me off.
BASIL:	(SLIGHT DISTORT) (CHUCKLES) Oh, tell him you're going to your grandmother's funeral.
ROGER:	Oh no. I couldn't possibly. Wouldn't dream of telling a lie.
BASIL:	(SLIGHT DISTORT) Oh, go on, force yourself.
ROGER:	No. It's against my principles. Couldn't possibly lie.
BASIL:	(SLIGHT DISTORT) But you do want to see the match?
ROGER:	Don't worry, I'll think of something. (PAUSE FOR TWO OR THREE SECONDS)

FX:	DOOR OPENS
ROGER:	(CALLS) (SOFTLY AND SWEETLY) Grannie! . . . Grannie! . . . Can you come here a moment?
GRANNIE:	(APPROACHING) Yes . . . What is it?
FX:	PISTOL SHOT.
	A HEAVY THUD AS BODY DROPS TO FLOOR
ROGER:	(INTO PHONE) Basil! It's all fixed. See you at the ground. What time's the kick off?

SOME TECHNICAL NOTES

The sketch opens with a sound effect, the phone ringing.

FX: is just a way of writing sound effects, that's all. Sound effects are either done live in the studio or they are on tape.

The person at the other end of the phone, Basil, is on slight distort, so that we know that he is on the other end. Without the slight distort it would sound as though Roger and Basil were in the same room together.

The sound effect of the door opening is usually done live in the studio. The pistol shot can be live or on tape. The effect of the heavy thud as the body falls to the floor would be on a prerecorded tape. The advantage of prerecording an effect is that the sound engineers have a chance to experiment, can offer the director several different choices and, of course, when the tape is played during the show you know exactly what you are going to get.

Television

Going from a radio studio to a television studio can be a bit of a shocker. In radio there are about half-a-dozen technicians in the studio, but in the TV studio there could be anything up to a hundred people involved in the production.

The average sitcom is recorded on four cameras –

Each camera shows a different picture –

The director cuts from one camera to another, first showing this picture then showing another.

Here is a simplified example of how four cameras are used:

If the set is a normal suburban house:

Camera no. 1 is in the hallway.
Camera no. 2 is in the front room.

Camera no. 3 is in the dining-room.
Camera no. 4 is in the kitchen.

The first shot is on Camera no. 1 – the husband, Fred, comes in through the front door.
The next shot is on Camera no. 4 – the wife is in the kitchen, hears Fred.
Then Camera no. 3 – in dining-room. Fred comes in. Wife comes in, says 'dinner not ready yet'.
Then cut to Camera no. 2 – Fred comes into front room and switches on telly.

Each camera shot is numbered, and there can be anything from up to 300 shots or more in a half-hour sitcom.

The director, not the writer, decides how to shoot the show. In effect, the director is saying to the audience, 'Now look at this, now look at that'. He decides which cameras to use and how to use them. He writes the information on the rehearsal script, which then becomes the camera script.

From rehearsal script to camera script
To get an idea of this process, here is an extract from a sitcom, *Take a Letter Mr Jones*. In this show – described in an earlier chapter – we have John Inman as Graham, personal secretary to a high-powered woman executive Mrs Warner, played by Rula Lenska. The producer/director was Bryan Izzard.

The situation in this extract is that Graham has bought some toys for Mrs Warner's young daughter – he wants a decision on the toys, but she is busy in a high level discussion with one of the bosses.

The scene is about a third of the way through the show, and we have reached camera shot **104**.

The Rehearsal Script

SCENE 13: INT MRS WAR-NER'S OFFICE

GRAHAM LOOKS IN. MRS WARNER AND BRADLEY HAVE THEIR LUNCH PLATES ON THE TABLE.

GRAHAM: Excuse me, Mrs Warner – could you spare a minute?

MRS WARNER: What is it, Graham? We are very busy.

GRAHAM: I need an important executive decision, and I'm afraid only you can make it.

MRS WARNER: What's it about, Graham?

GRAHAM: It's very confidential.

MRS WARNER GETS UP AND GOES INTO GRAHAM'S OFFICE.

END OF SCENE 13

The Camera Script

SCENE 13: INT MRS WAR-
NER'S OFFICE

104 4 (A) M2S MRS
           WARNER & MR
           BRADLEY

           SEE GRAHAM
           ENTER L.

GRAHAM LOOKS IN. MRS
WARNER AND BRADLEY HAVE
THEIR LUNCH PLATES ON THE
TABLE.

GRAHAM: Excuse me, Mrs
Warner – could you spare a
minute?

MRS WARNER: What is it,
Graham? We are very busy.

(104/4)

GRAHAM: I need an impor-
tant executive decision, and I'm
afraid only you can make it.

MRS WARNER: What's it
about, Graham?

GRAHAM: It's very con-
fidential.

MRS WARNER GETS UP AND GOES
INTO GRAHAM'S OFFICE.

END OF SCENE 13

SCEME 14: INT GRAHAM'S OFFICE

MRS WARNER: Well, what is it?

GRAHAM: (INDICATING PACKAGES) You've got to decide which of these presents you want for Lucy.

MRS WARNER: (AMAZED) I'm in my office discussing a half-million pound budget with Mr Bradley and you drag me out here for that?!!

GRAHAM: Well, I'm not the girl's mother, am I? It was all so confusing. There were thousands of different toys to choose from – space games – robots – dolls from outer space – electronic dolls – not to mention Ludo.

MRS WARNER: All right – calm down. What did you get?

GRAHAM OPENS ONE PLASTIC BAG AND BRINGS OUT A HUGE TEDDY BEAR.

MRS WARNER: (AMAZED) A teddy bear?! Why on earth did you get that? No child of seven would want a teddy bear!

GRAHAM: I had one when I was seven. I've still got it!

MRS WARNER: Well, Lucy is very advanced for her age.

GRAHAM LOOKS IN ANOTHER BAG.

105 2 (B)	MS AS GRAHAM & MRS WARNER ENTER GRAHAM'S OFFICE & COME DOWN TO TOYS.

SCENE 14:   INT GRAHAM'S OFFICE

MRS WARNER: Well, what is it?

GRAHAM: (INDICATING PACKAGES) You've got to decide which of these presents you want for Lucy.

106 1 (A)   CU MRS WARNER

MRS WARNER: (AMAZED) I'm in my office discussing a half-million pound budget with Mr Bradley and you drag me out here for that?!!

107 3 (A)   CU GRAHAM

GRAHAM: Well, I'm not the girl's mother, am I? It was all so confusing. There were thousands of different toys to choose from – space games – robots – dolls from outer space – electronic dolls – not to mention Ludo.

108 2 (B)   M2S A/B

MRS WARNER: All right – calm down. What did you get?

GRAHAM OPENS ONE PLASTIC BAG AND BRINGS OUT A HUGE TEDDY BEAR.

MRS WARNER: (AMAZED) A teddy bear?! Why on earth did

109 1 (A)   CU MRS WARNER

you get that? No child of seven would want a teddy bear!

110 3 (A)   CU GRAHAM A/B

GRAHAM: I had one when I was seven. I've still got it!

111 1 (A)   CU MRS WARNER

MRS WARNER: Well, Lucy is very advanced for her age.

112 2 (B)   M2S A/B

GRAHAM LOOKS IN ANOTHER BAG.

GRAHAM: Oh well, you'll like this then.

HE BRINGS OUT A RADIO-CONTROLLED ROBOT. A SMALL VERSION OF R2D2.

MRS WARNER: A robot? What would a little girl want with that?

GRAHAM: You just said she was advanced. This is the latest model – he's controlled by a silicon chip. Look . . .

HE PULLS THE RADIO CONTROL BOX OUT OF THE BAG AND PRESSES A BUTTON OR TWIRLS A LEVER. THE ROBOT MOVES FOR-WARD AND TURNS AT HIS COMMAND.

GRAHAM: Great, isn't it? Just press the buttons and it does everything you want. Just like me.

MRS WARNER: (IMPATIEN-TLY) No, no. Lucy wouldn't like that. What is in the other bag?

GRAHAM: It's a doll.

HE BRINGS OUT A LARGE, EXPENSIVE-LOOKING BABY DOLL.

MRS WARNER: I suppose that might do – but she's already got several dolls.

GRAHAM: This is the latest one – very lifelike. It drinks milk from a bottle, makes rumbling noises, and if you press it, it does all sorts of other revolting things.

GRAHAM: Oh well, you'll like this then.

HE BRINGS OUT A RADIO-CONTROLLED ROBOT. A SMALL VERSION OF R2D2.

MRS WARNER: A robot? What would a little girl want with that?

GRAHAM: You just said she was advanced. This is the latest model – he's controlled by a silicon chip. Look . . .

HE PULLS THE RADIO CONTROL BOX OUT OF THE BAG AND PRESSES A BUTTON OR TWIRLS A LEVER. THE ROBOT MOVES FORWARD AND TURNS AT HIS COMMAND.

113 1 (A)   CU ROBOT

113 3 (A)   CU GRAHAM AB

GRAHAM: Great, isn't it? Just press the buttons and it does everything you want. Just like me.

115 2 (B)   M2S A/B

MRS WARNER: (IMPATIENTLY) No, no. Lucy wouldn't like that. What is in the other bag?

GRAHAM: It's a doll.

HE BRINGS OUT A LARGE, EXPENSIVE-LOOKING BABY DOLL.

MRS WARNER: I suppose that might do – but she's already got several dolls.

115a 3 (A)   CU DOLL
             PAN UP TO
             GRAHAM

GRAHAM: This is the latest one — very lifelike. It drinks milk from a bottle, makes rumbling noises, and if you press it, it does all sorts of other revolting things.

116 1 (A)   CU MRS WARNER

MRS WARNER: Such as what?

GRAHAM: I can't tell you, but when I was coming back in the lift, people pressed right up against the parcel, and it did it! I shall have to buy a new raincoat.

MRS WARNER: All right. We'll settle for the doll. Wrap it up, and return the other things. I must get back to Mr Bradley.

SHE GOES OUT.

END OF SCENE 14

MRS   WARNER: Such   as
what?

117 3 (A)   CU GRAHAM

GRAHAM: I can't tell you,
but when I was coming back in
the life, people pressed right up
against the parcel, and it did it! I
shall have to buy a new
raincoat.

118 2 (B)   M2S A/B

MRS   WARNER: All   right.
We'll settle for the doll. Wrap it
up, and return the other things.
I must get back to Mr Bradley.

LOOSEN AS MRS
WARNER GOES
TO HER DOOR.
STAY WITH
GRAHAM AS SHE
GOES OUT.

SHE GOES OUT.

END OF SCENE 14

SOME NOTES ON THE CAMERA SCRIPT

<u>104 4 (A)</u>	We are on shot 104 of the show – this shot is being taken by Camera 4.
	And Camera 4 is in position A. (Cameras are moved to different positions during the show. A, B, C, D, etc.)
<u>M2S MRS WARNER</u> <u>MR BRADLEY</u>	Medium Two shot – of Mrs Warner and Mr Bradley.
<u>GRAHAM ENTERS L</u>	Graham enters from left, i.e. cameraman's left.
<u>M2S A/B</u>	Medium Two shot as before.

Notice that between shot 115 and 116, a new shot has been added – 115a. The director obviously decided an extra shot was needed and it was added in after the technical run through.

<u>PAN UP TO GRAHAM</u>	Pan up is to tilt the camera up.
<u>LOOSEN AS</u>	The camera pulls back to a wider shot to include the door.
<u>MRS WARNER</u> <u>GOES TO HER DOOR</u>	

THE DIRECTOR, NOT THE WRITER, DECIDES HOW THE SCRIPT WILL BE SHOT
Therefore there should be the closest co-operation, understanding and empathy between director and writer.

Even so, there are always times when the final shots are not quite like the writer imagined.

It is a tremendous advantage if the writer, or one of the writers, is also the director, such as David Croft or Dick Clement.

Films
Exterior scenes in television shows:
  In television shows, exterior scenes such as a car going
down the road . . . meeting at a railway station . . . are filmed
and then inserted when the show is recorded.
  The filming technique used in these inserts is the same
technique as in feature films.
  One camera is used and is moved from position to
position, and each position is called a set up.

Film makers have developed a language of their own, and
below are some of the terms which you ought to know:

A take	A shot or scene of any length shot without stopping the camera.
Dissolve	When one scene merges into another – often used to denote a passing of time. In television, this is called a MIX.
Pan camera	Rotate camera to the left or the right, or tilt up or down.
P.O.V.	POINT OF VIEW – if you want a shot of a helicopter as your character FRED sees it, you write: EXT: AIR STRIP HELICOPTER LANDING FRED'S P.O.V.
Tracking shot	This is usually done with the camera pushed along on specially laid tracks. If FRED is walking across the field, then in a tracking shot, the camera moves with him, alongside him.
Reverse shot	A take repeated with camera facing the other way. For example: If we have a shot of FRED going to greet the PILOT, the reverse shot would be over the PILOT'S SHOULDER as he sees FRED approach.

In filming and in television, there are no end of tricks

available to the director, maybe too many.

In drama, the director may go in for quick cutting, long panning shots, overhead shots, shots at crazy angles, odd lightning effects, and so on. These tricks have no place in comedy.

In the best comedy the audience should not be aware of direction.

The best examples are the Woody Allen films where the takes are sometimes quite long, the camera does not jump around, and there are no tricks even to denote the passing of time. Woody Allen is not frightened to go to black for a brief second.

As a general rule in films and television, comedy should be shot as it would normally be seen, i.e. if a comedy scene is taking place around a dining-table, the audience should feel as if they are in the room watching the scene at roughly the same eye-level as the actors, not perched on a swinging chandelier looking down at them.

New writers will obviously pick up more technical terms as they go along.

But on your first time in a TV studio, be careful – there are live microphones everywhere.

If you are in a control room with a director, be wary of making any unkind remarks about the camera crew. These will be picked up and heard not just by all the technicians in your studio, but by many others all the way down the line.

Be even more cautious when you are on the floor, or on the set talking to actors. A chance remark such as: 'That flipping director has got no bloody idea – he's ruining my script', will probably be heard by the director through one of the live mikes, and is not likely to further your career.

Independent TV companies
who produce comedy

CELADOR PRODUCTIONS LTD
(Jasper Carrott shows; *The Detectives*, with Jasper Carrott
and Robert Powell; *Who Wants to be a Millionaire*)
39 Long Acre
London WC2E 9JT
Tel: 020 7240 8101
Fax: 020 7836 1117
Contact: Paul Smith

CHANNEL X
(Jonathan Ross; Jo Brand – *Through the Cakehole*; *Smell of
Reeves & Mortimer*)
Middlesex House
32-42 Cleveland Street
London W1P 5FB
Tel: 020 7436 2200
Fax: 020 7436 1475

CINEMA VERITY
(*May to December*; *So Haunt Me*; *A Class Act*, with Joanna
Lumley)
The Mill House
Millers Way
1a Shepherd's Bush Road
London W6 7NA
Tel: 020 8749 8485
Fax: 020 8743 5062
Contact: Verity Lambert, Sharon Bloom

HARTSWOOD FILMS LTD
(*Men Behaving Badly*; *Is It Legal?*; *Coupling*)
Shepperton Studios
Shepperton
Middlesex TW17 0QD
Tel: 01932 572294
Fax: 01932 572299
Contact: Beryl Vertue, Elaine Cameron

HAT TRICK PRODUCTIONS LTD
(*Drop the Dead Donkey*; Paul Merton series; *Clive Anderson Talks Back*)
10 Livonia Street
London W1V 3PH
Tel: 020 7434 2451
Fax: 020 7287 9791
Contact: Denise O'Donoghue

HIGHTIME PRODUCTIONS LTD
(*Me & My Girl*)
5 Angler's Lane
Kentish Town
London NW5 3DG
Tel: 020 7482 5202
Fax: 020 7485 4254
Contact: A.C. Mitchell, A. Humphries

PLANET 24
(*The Big Breakfast*; *The Word*)
The Planet Building
Thames Quay
195 Marsh Wall
London E14 9SG
Tel: 020 7345 2424
Fax: 020 7345 9400
Contact: Tracey Macleod

SELECTV plc is a writer-led production company comprising Alomo (Marks and Gran), Clement/La Frenais and Witzend productions. They produce drama and comedy.
(*Goodnight Sweetheart*; *Birds of a Feather*; *Pie in the Sky*; *New Statesman*; Tracey Ullman)
Pearson Television
1 Stephen Street
London W1P 1PJ
Tel: 020 7691 6000

TALKBACK PRODUCTIONS
Formed in 1981 by Mel Smith and Griff Rhys Jones.
(*Smith and Jones*; *Murder Most Horrid*; *The Day Today*; *Knowing Me, Knowing You* with Alan Partridge)
36 Percy Street
London W1P 0LN
Tel: 020 7323 9777
Fax: 020 7637 5105
Contact: Peter Fincham

THAMES TELEVISION INTERNATIONAL LTD
UK's largest independent production company
Broom Road
Teddington Lock
Middlesex TW11 9NT
Tel: 020 8614 2800
Contact: Phil Morrow

TIGER ASPECT PRODUCTIONS
(*Mr Bean*; *The Vicar of Dibley*; *Paul Merton's Life of Comedy*)
5 Soho Square
London W1V 5DE
Tel: 020 7434 0672
Fax: 020 7287 1448
Contact: Charles Brand

WARNER SISTERS
(*Dressing for Breakfast*)
Camelot Studios
222 Kensal Road
London W10 5BN
Tel: 020 8960 3550
Contact: Lavinia Warner

WORKING TITLE FILMS LTD
(Films: *The Tall Guy*; *Four Weddings and a Funeral* Television:
The Baldy Man; *The Borrowers*; *Tales of the City*)
Oxford House
76 Oxford Street
London W1N 9FD
Tel: 020 7307 3000
Fax: 020 7307 3001
Contact: Films – Tim Bevan; Television – Simon Wright

Index